The Village of Chelm's Pond – centrally isolated in New York's Adirondack Mountains, just north of Blue Mountain Lake between Castle Rock and Little Blue Mountain, the steep valley where every acre is two acres, you can till the soil with a teaspoon, and there are not only four seasons, there are five.

Adirondack Mendel's Aufruf

Welcome to Chelm's Pond

Sandor Schuman

Illustrated by Kevin Kuhne

6/14/2018

To Claire and Arnold,

The first to reach out to us — and much appreciated.

Enjoy this little gem!

Pie and Miriam

© 2012 by Sandor Schuman. All rights reserved.
www.chelmspond.com
sschuman@exedes.com

This Too Shall Pass Press
Albany, New York

Table of Contents

Acknowledgments	1
Preface	3
Chelm's Pond	5
Rabbi Chayim Shmayim	9
The Village Council	13
Bloomie	19
Diner Slang	23
Geneva Bus Stop	25
The Rabbi's Hat	29
The Way to Paradise	33
The Broiled Beet	45
Adirondack Mendel	51
Deception	53
The Fly Fishing Contest	57
Castle Rock	63
Aufruf the Dog	69
Adirondack Mendel Tells the Truth	73
Economic Development	79
Conversion	83
Respect	93
Sim Shalom - שִׂימ שָׁלוֹם	103
Glossary	105
Adirondack Mendel's Study Guide	115
About the Author and Illustrator	119

Acknowledgments

My cousin, Susan Barnett Wood, a technical writer and editor, reviewed an early version of the book and made numerous content and style suggestions. She agreed that this was a "collection of stories," but also an overall story that is more than the sum of its parts. I hope she is right.

Robyn Ringler, writer, editor, and owner of East Line Books, examined a late version of the book and provided detailed feedback. She told me how, at a family dinner, the stories got a lot of laughs and some serious reflection. What more could I want?

For the trick questions foisted upon Adirondack Mendel by the Chelmites I thank my sister, Selma Aaronson, former Hebrew school teacher and principal. I hope her former students have figured out which direction to face when gossiping.

My oldest sister, Sheila Ornstein, enlightened me on many Yiddish and Hebrew language issues. For example, I called her late one night to ask, "Would you say *shoyn genug*, or *genug shoyn*?" After reading the whole manuscript, she said, "You know, it gets more serious at the end. It's like bait and switch."

At a Shabbat Kiddush, I asked the following question of Rabbi Robert Fine, then Interim Rabbi at Temple Israel of Albany: "Can an atheist convert to Judaism and still be an atheist?" That conversation, supplemented by follow-up emails and additional conversations with Rabbi Daniel Ornstein at Congregation Ohav Shalom (yes, he is related to my sister Sheila – he's her son), laid the foundation for the *Conversion* chapter. In addition, both of these rabbis reviewed the entire manuscript and made helpful suggestions. I would like to claim that the whole process has been conducted under strict rabbinical supervision.

At one of his Thursday night classes on "Prayer: Problem or Possibility," Temple Israel's Rabbi David Eligberg shared with us the collection of sticky notes he has accumulated in his *siddur*, each with an insight, question, or commentary. One of them, "The prayer changes the prayer," stimulated a lot of discussion. They are still talking about it in Chelm's Pond.

Chaim Picker, Temple Israel's Cantor Emeritus, author, poet, teacher, and my tutor on Shabbat mornings, pointed out some inconsistencies in the manuscript not noticed by others. For example, he asked, "How could the *Sephardic* grandfather have an *Ashkenazic* name?" To find out how I addressed this issue, you'll have to read the story.

After telling some Chelm's Pond stories at a Temple Israel Men's Club breakfast, Dr. Joseph Adler offered a suggestion. "The dog's name should be Aufruf." With a name like that, he had to become a major character. Aufruf thanks you, Bloomie and Adirondack Mendel thank you, and I thank you.

My son Benjamin gave me a useful piece of advice. "Don't kill the punch line." This proved to be something of a challenge for me, especially as I incorporated jokes into the context of a larger story. I hope I can qualify for the disclaimer, "No punch lines were harmed in the telling of this story." You be the judge.

I was *farklempt* when I first saw Kevin Kuhne's illustration of Bloomie inside the Broiled Beet. The sun reflected off Chelm's Pond and lit up Little Blue Mountain, visible through the windows of the café. Kevin brought Chelm's Pond and its characters to life. Business at the Broiled Beet has been booming ever since.

My wife, Martha Healy, would not want me to mention her here, although her comments, suggestions, and encouragement are reflected throughout (not to mention that she gets credit for the poem, *Promise*). She would probably say, "Acknowledgment shmowledgment, publish the book already!"

Lastly, I owe a debt of gratitude to Rabbi Joseph Schevelowitz, *zekher tzadik livrakha*. As part of my Bar Mitzvah preparation, he taught me to lead the *Musaph* service and sing *Sim Shalom*, which I have come to appreciate as the summary of all the prayers that precede it, the grand finale of the entire service, and the greatest plea. If only it would work.

Preface

Is there anything special about Jewish stories? Perhaps they are just like the stories of other cultural traditions. But if there is a difference, what is it that makes a story distinctively *Jewish*?

I thought I would explore this original question – until I discovered that it wasn't so original, that others had already asked the question and given thoughtful answers, writing about unique aspects of Jewish folktales, jokes, and humor.[1] Among all those explanations and descriptions, the most satisfying definition I found was this:

> A *Jewish* story is one that a non-Jew wouldn't understand, and a Jewish person has already heard.

Admittedly, this book incorporates some old Jewish stories and jokes, though presented in a new way. If you are Jewish, but don't know these stories, then by the above definition, this book amounts to required reading. Read on so you too can say "Yeah, I heard it before" (and then tell your version, which is, of course, better). If you are not Jewish (and even if you are), and the story does not make sense – for you, I will explain.

This book has footnotes and a glossary. Pretty sophisticated for a book that is, *takkeh,* supposed to be humorous. Yiddish and Hebrew words and phrases are italicized and explained in the glossary. Some additional explanations appear in *Adiron-*

---

[1] For example: Nathan Ausubel, Editor, *A Treasury of Jewish Folklore: Stories, Traditions, Legends, Humor, Wisdom and Folk Songs of the Jewish People.* Crown, 1948, pp. xx-xxi. Henry Eilbert, *What is a Jewish Joke: An Excursion into Jewish Humor.* Jason Aaronson, 1981, pp. 59-61. William Novak and Moshe Waldoks, Editors, *The Big Book of Jewish Humor.* Harper Perennial, 1981, pp. xx-xxii. Dov Noy, "Forward: What is Jewish about the Jewish Folktale." In, Howard Schwartz, *Miriam's Tambourine: Jewish Folktales from Around the World.* Oxford University Press, 1988, pp. xv-xviii. Rabbi Joseph Telushkin, *Jewish Humor: What the Best Jewish Jokes Say About the Jews.* William Morrow, 1992, pp. 16-17.

dack Mendel's Study Guide. To ask questions, make suggestions, and find additional information, please visit www.exedes.com/chelm's-pond.

Sandor (Sandy) Schuman
November, 2012
Albany, New York

Chelm's Pond

Some people are so confident of their wisdom
they are unaware of their foolishness.

The legendary Jews of Chelm were reluctant to leave behind their beloved, ancestral home of Chelm, Poland. But they were offered an irresistible land deal in America. The real estate agent raved about the land, assuring them that in this wonderful tract "every acre is two acres, you can till the soil with a teaspoon, and there are not only four seasons, there are five." To their further astonishment, the broker announced that it included a fifteen-acre body of water named Chelm's Pond (although he admitted – in an effort to demonstrate his honesty – that it appears on maps with an anglicized spelling, "Helms Pond"). Surely, the move to Chelm's Pond was *bashert.*

While some were skeptical of the real estate agent's claims, they discovered upon their arrival that every word was true! Every acre was two acres because the hills and mountain sides were so steep – if flattened out, they would double the acreage. You could till the soil with a teaspoon because the soil was so shallow. And there were not only four seasons, there were five: summer, fall, winter, spring, and black fly season, the "fifth season."[2]

---

[2] From late May through most of June the Adirondacks are dominated by huge numbers of black flies that feast on humans, their painful bites leaving itchy, red sores. These tiny insects so change the character of the Adirondacks that the locals refer to this time period as "black fly season," or "the fifth season."

Assured that their wisdom had prevailed and that they received what they paid for, the people of Chelm settled in. They built homes, a *shul*, farmed, traded, married, had children and grandchildren, carried on their traditions, and lived in Chelmudic bliss in this remote, roadless valley, accessible only by hiking miles of unmarked trails, sheltered and unknown to the rest of the world.

How did I come by this knowledge? I was hiking in New York State's Adirondack Mountains and I got lost. There were no roads or trails, no telephone poles, no cell phone signals. I was in the middle of nowhere. That's when I stumbled into Chelm's Pond. The Chelmites welcomed me into their little village and eagerly shared their personal and communal history. Each time I met one of them it was like we were old friends and when we parted they wished me *zay gezunt*, and it was not said as a mere formality or a social platitude, they really meant it.

While there, I witnessed an extraordinary thing such as no one has ever seen or heard before and some might not have believed even if they did. Was it for real? Well, I wish you could have been there so you could have judged for yourself because, you see, some people said it really happened, but others said it was just another tall tale.

It happened at Adirondack Mendel's *aufruf*. No, not his talking dog, Aufruf, his *aufruf!* Adirondack Mendel was going to marry Bloomie, the ambitious proprietor of The Broiled Beet (serving the finest in Adirondack-Ashkenazick fusion cuisine), and in all of Chelm's Pond the loveliest, kindest, and sincerest *sheyne meydl*. It was during his *aufruf* – when he was called up to the *Torah* on the *Shabbos* before the wedding – when the learned, honored, and beloved Rabbi Chayim Shmayim, the oldest and wisest *khokhem* in Chelm's Pond, was concluding the *musaph* service.

What's that you say, "*hock mir nisht kayn chaynik.*" You want me I should stop beating around the bush and say what happened? Well I could tell you, but I assure you it wouldn't make any sense unless you had a thorough understanding of the nature of this remarkable village, the reputations of these individuals in the community, the historical, cultural, philosophical, sociological, and economic context – the *gantzeh megillah*. Are you ready?

Here is what's news from Chelm's Pond, centrally isolated in New York's Adirondack Mountains, just north of Blue Mountain Lake between Castle Rock and Little Blue Mountain, the steep valley where every acre is two acres, where you can till the soil with a teaspoon, and there are not only four seasons, there are five.

Rabbi Chayim Shmayim

An understanding of the community could not be achieved without at least a brief introduction to the learned, honored, and beloved Rabbi Chayim Tzvi, the oldest and wisest *khokhem* in Chelm's Pond.

Rabbi Chayim Tzvi could be relied on to find a solution to even the most vexing problem. For example, he once received a letter from Frank, an ex-Chelmite, with an offer to donate $10,000 to the *shul's* building fund. With the *shul* in such a sad state of disrepair – people tripped over the buckets that collected drips from the leaky roof, flames licked through the rusted holes of the wood stove, the glare of sunlight through the chimney made you squint, the spongy floorboards made you feel seasick – this was a much needed gift.

Frank and his older brother John were Chelmites of dubious reputations. The brothers spurned Jewish culture and abandoned their *Yiddishe* names, refused to participate in or support any community or religious events and, while they never hesitated to ask their Chelmite neighbors for favors, could never be relied upon to help others, even when asked. By stroke of good fortune – a mystery of providence – they had many years ago won $1,300 in the New York State Lottery. On hearing the news, Frank yelled "Yahoo!" John took this as a sign and used the winnings to buy 1,000 shares of stock in an upstart Internet company with the ridiculous name *Yahoo!* They sold the stock four years later at $500 per share and left Chelm's Pond without sharing a penny of their good fortune with their fellow Chelmites.

No one in Chelm's Pond heard anything from them until Rabbi Chayim Tzvi received Frank's letter with the offer of a gift of $10,000. But the offer came with a strict condition. Frank's elder brother John had died, and Frank wanted the rabbi to speak at the memorial service. His letter insisted, "In the eulogy you must say, 'He was a *mensh.*' No other wording will be acceptable."

How could Rabbi Chayim Tzvi, an honorable and trustworthy man, say of the older brother John that "he was a *mensh?*" The brothers, in their own narrow self interests, would turn on a friend, cheat a relative, misdirect an unwitting stranger. And yet, the community could greatly benefit from the repairs the money would buy.

He looked to heaven for inspiration. He didn't merely gaze toward the sky, his penetrating stare had such intensity that his whole face inclined upwards, his chin pointing towards heaven and skewed to the right in such an extreme posture that you would consider it an unnatural feat of acrobatics, and with such yearning that he would inevitably rise on his right foot, extending his toes to get even that much closer to heaven. And as he stood so outstretched, he would after a few moments lose his balance, and to prevent himself from falling over he crossed his left foot over his right, taking a step in that direction, all the while looking up and to his right, his eyes reaching out to heaven. Every few minutes the pattern would repeat, an awkward image, oblivious to his surroundings, haphazardly hobbling diagonally to his right as he sought heavenly inspiration. From this behavior, imploring heaven, he earned the Chelmudic distinction, "Rabbi Chayim who looks to *shamayim.*" But most people just called him "Rabbi Chayim Shmayim."[3]

Rabbi Chayim Shmayim maintained this dynamic pose for three days, during which time the people of Chelm's Pond never doubted that their learned, honored, and beloved rabbi, the

---

[3] Repeating a word with the first sound replaced by "shm" is a Yiddish device for making light of or diminishing the idea. Examples of this device adopted in English are "fancy shmancy" and "Joe Shmo."

oldest and wisest *khokhem* in Chelm's Pond, would achieve the inspiration that would allow him to accept the much-needed gift of $10,000. After three days of beseeching heaven he fell into a deep sleep. He dreamt that he received a box of chocolate candies. He tasted one, but didn't like it. He sampled a second, but liked it less than the first. The third he liked less than the second, and so on, each candy less to his liking than the previous. Compared to the subsequent candies, the first one was a treat! Suddenly, he woke up, the problem solved.

The day of the memorial service arrived and everyone in Chelm's Pond attended, eager to hear how the rabbi would accept the $10,000 gift and maintain his integrity while making reference to John with the words, "He was a *mensh*."

In his eulogy, delivered in the dilapidated *shul* to the anxious assembly of Chelmites, Rabbi Chayim Shmayim said, "Never in the history of this community was there ever a person who was less concerned about the well-being of his fellow man." These words created a mild state of alarm among the Chelmites as they began to question their rabbi's intent. "Among all the people of Chelm's Pond," he continued, "never has there been anyone less truthful, less trusting, or less trustworthy." The Chelmites' hopes sank as their anticipated receipt of the surviving brother's $10,000 gift oozed away like beet borsht spilled on a white cotton tablecloth. "Any of us," the rabbi's voice rang out, "is more reliable, more helpful, more decent, more worthy of admiration."

The despairing Chelmites began to shuffle toward the door, their anticipated gain evaporating like steam from boiled potatoes. "But compared to his brother," concluded Rabbi Chayim Shmayim in a steady, declarative tone, "he was a *mensh!*"

Such is the indefatigable wisdom of Rabbi Chayim Shmayim, who figures so prominently in the life of Chelm's Pond. However, lest you think this little story provides a sufficient basis for your understanding of Chelm's Pond, I must hasten to introduce you to some of the other individuals essential to this tale.

The Village Council

To give you some insight into the nature of Chelm's Pond and its people, their interpersonal dynamics, group decision-making processes, and respect for tradition, there would be no better way than to share with you the story of the village water supply and how it was made safe for all of the inhabitants.

It was a dark day, of overcast sky as well as grim mood, when young Moishe – a three-year-old innocent child, a lovely, sweet boy – suddenly disappeared. The entire village turned out to search for him. And find him they did, to his parents' and the whole village's relief, floating in a bucket at the bottom of the well on the outskirts of the village. It was Bloomie who found him and calmed him and told him everything would be all right and ran to get help. It was Bloomie who bravely agreed to have a rope tied to her ankles and was lowered down into the damp darkness to retrieve the child. And it was Bloomie to whom young Moishe clung as a raw egg to a hot, un-greased frying pan. But it was the thorough, thoughtful, and decisive Chelm's Pond Village Council that vowed such a near-tragedy would never happen again.

"We must take action immediately," Herschel implored the council, "to ensure that such a thing can never happen again. We must protect our citizens from the dangers of the well. Let's build a stone wall around the well so a small child can't fall in." The members of the village council immediately set to work and a four-foot stone wall around the well was soon completed.

"Wait, the stone wall isn't enough. What about the adults?" Golda asked. "If they leaned over the stone wall they could fall into the well. It could happen! Let's put up warning signs." Each member of the village council made a sign or two, fastened each to a post, and drove the post into the ground. Within minutes the well was surrounded by signs. Some were straightforward but generic: "Proceed with Caution," "Danger," "Watch Your Step." Some were more specific but cryptic: "Well," "Hole in the Ground," "Your Next Step May Be Your Last."

The sign voted "most clever" was Herschel's:

> To keep your head well,
> keep your head well out of
> the wellhead ahead.

Golda's was voted "most poetic:"

> Little Moishe fell into the well.
> He was there for a spell with no one to tell.
> He was saved by a belle and now all is swell.
> But be careful because you might not be so lucky.

Raizel won for "best use of local fauna:"

> Turtles have a shell
> Chelm's Pond has a well
> You would get hurt
> If in it you fell.

Shlomo won in the "couplet, ten words or less" category:

> Beware where you dwell
> Don't fall in the well.

No sooner had the signs been installed than Malka pointed out what should have been already obvious. "The signs aren't enough. What if a person who is visually impaired walks by and can't read the signs, or someone comes by in the dark of night? They won't see the signs and they could stumble over the wall and fall into the well. It's unlikely to happen, but it could! We must keep people from falling into the well. We should hire someone to read the signs out loud and shine a flashlight on the signs at night." The village council adopted this measure unanimously and hired Shaindel, who went to work immediately at this most important job.

Shlomo was comforted by this decision, but then he found new worries. "What if Shaindel should fall asleep on the job? It's possible! There would be no one to read the signs to the visually impaired or shine a flashlight on the signs in the dark. We must keep people from falling into the well. We should build a fence around it." No sooner had Shlomo finished than his wisdom was acknowledged and a fence was ordered to surround the area.

The members of the village council gathered to admire their work. They looked upon the well with its stout stone wall, the warning signs facing out in every direction, the new tall fence continuously patrolled by Shaindel, who read aloud the signs in her vibrant, piercing voice, flashlight ready for nightfall. Reflecting on each of their contributions, Herschel declared, "None of us is as smart as all of us."

As they congratulated each other on their collective wisdom and decisive actions, they saw Fieval approach to fill his water jug at the well. Seeing the fence, he scratched his head and went away, returning soon with a ladder. He set the ladder against the fence, climbed over, exchanged pleasantries with Shaindel, weaved his way between the signs, and filled his jug with water. "What are we to do now," cried Herschel. "What if someone like Fieval should bring a ladder and forget it there, and someone else will come at night, climb the ladder, find Shaindel asleep, and fall into the well?

What could they do to prevent such a calamity? In a collective insight they all shouted "Close the well!" This was an excellent solution. But after a moment's reflection they realized it posed a new problem. "How will we get water?" Desperate for a resolution to this knotty problem, they called upon their learned, honored, and beloved Rabbi Chayim Shmayim, the oldest and wisest *khokhem* in Chelm's Pond.

True to his reputation, Rabbi Chayim Shmayim launched himself into finding a solution for this critical community problem. From the extended toes of his right foot to the outstretched hand and fingers of his right arm, his entire body strove toward heaven in his quest for an answer. As he could not maintain his balance in this position, he began to fall to his right and thus his left leg came across to keep him from falling, every few minutes repeating this awkward locomotion. After three days, he fell asleep. He had a dream.

In the dream, it was a hot and muggy day. Little Moishe was sweating uncomfortably in his chair at one end of a long table and far at the other end was a tall glass of ice-cold *esrog*ade, the moisture in the air condensing on the glass, forming small droplets and bigger droplets that ran down to the table. Little Moishe wanted that refreshing *esrog*ade, but stretch as he might, he couldn't reach it. He held a straw in his mouth and the straw grew longer and longer until it reached across the table to the bottom of the glass. He drank through that straw and, making that sucking-straw-at-the-bottom-of-the-glass sound, drained every last drop of *esrog*ade.

The Rabbi woke up and gathered everyone around to hear his solution. "Yes, you should fill in the well and close up the hole, but before you do, dig a trench from the well to the center of the village. Lay a pipe along the bottom of the trench from the well to the center of the village, where you will install a water pump. Then, cover the trench with soil. The water pump will be more convenient to everyone, and no one will be able to fall into the well because there won't be a hole in the ground, only a one-inch diameter pipe buried in the ground."

"That's a wonderful solution," exclaimed Herschel.

"Excellent," cried Shlomo. "Now we can take down the stone wall, remove the signs and the fence, and we don't have to continue paying Shaindel."

"Oh no," said Rabbi Chayim Shmayim, "I would not advise that. You should keep all those measures in place."

Fartumelt, Raizel blurted, "But Rabbi, once we install the new water pump in the center of the village, those other things won't serve a purpose anymore!"

"Ah, but they were all good things in their time," Rabbi Chayim Shmayim responded, "and they will serve to remind us of our history and traditions, so we should keep them." All of the members of the village council recognized his wisdom and nodded in agreement.

To this day, if you should visit Chelm's Pond and go to the edge of the village, there you will find Shaindel, patrolling the fence that encloses the warning signs that surround the stone wall that blocks the well, which was filled in and closed. It is a very safe well indeed.

BLOOMIE

While many people see the members of the village council as the heroes and heroines in the story of the village well, some see Rabbi Chayim Shmayim as the hero. But whenever he heard such talk he was always quick to point out that the bigger hero – or heroine in this case – was actually Bloomie. Although others rarely gave her credit, Rabbi Chayim Shmayim always gave credit where it was due. The scale on which he assessed people measured only their merits, not their faults, just as it says in the *Pirke Avos*.[4] And he was especially fond and protective of Bloomie. As she figures prominently in the events of Adirondack Mendel's *aufruf*, it is important that you meet her.

When she was a youngster, her awkward appearance and unconventional manners produced many smiles and oft-retold stories, none flattering. She was funny to look at and funnier to tell about, but her actions were always well intentioned, even if poorly executed. In high school, as she matured, the boys of Chelm's Pond would gaze at her absent-mindedly, her athletic build and tender facial expression causing many a young lad to *fargesn* his lesson. A real *sheyne meydl, a gutte neshomeh*, she was beautiful inside and out. She loved everything and everyone.

However, even by Chelm's Pond standards, she was – how can I say this politely – cognitively challenged. The children –

---

[4] *Pirke Avos* 1:6, "Yehoshua ben Perahyah said: Provide yourself with a teacher; acquire a friend; and judge every person in the scale of merit."

and the boys in particular – often made fun of her. In another community they might have said "she is not the sharpest knife in the drawer," or "she only has one oar in the water," or "she is all foam and no beer." But in Chelm's Pond they would say, "she couldn't find the hole in a bagel," "she couldn't cut *gefilte* fish with a sharp knife," "her *khallah* is missing a braid," or "she could buy *tefillin* at half price." When they said "she can light up a room," they meant she could accidentally set something on fire. When she left the room, they joked that it was like an interesting person walked in.

As a young woman, she matured in her perspective and understanding of the world, but felt constrained by her own past – knowing how the people of Chelm's Pond remembered her.

Enough already with generalities. To really understand Bloomie and her place in the community, a few examples from her past will be necessary.

Diner Slang

Bloomie's parents, Shlomo and Raizel, scratched together a living as owners of the only retail establishment in Chelm's Pond, a general store and trading post that included the only eatery in Chelm's Pond, a small diner, in which they took great pride. Of their abilities as cooks it was often said that Raizel's refined palate could readily distinguish between sweet and sour; Shlomo could tell hot from cold. When she was a little girl, Bloomie helped out by sweeping the floor and cleaning tables, and when she got older she waited on tables while her mother focused on cooking and her father ran the general store. Raised in this secluded community, and forever seeking knowledge of the larger world, Bloomie made it her mission, through extraordinary effort, to bring worldly standards – and taste – to the diner.

On a rare trip with her family to nearby Indian Lake, she insisted that they stop in the local diner to see how a "real eating establishment" operates. Bloomie was fascinated when the waitress quietly took an order from one of the customers and then, while writing the order on the customer's check, turned her head over her shoulder and called into the kitchen, "BLT down, heavy on the mayo," which, Bloomie learned, meant "a bacon, lettuce, and tomato sandwich on toast (that's what 'down' meant, as in pushing down on the toaster handle to send the bread into the toaster) with a lot of mayonnaise." For another customer the waitress called "two sunny-side up, burnt British in the alley," which, Bloomie learned, meant "two fried eggs with unbroken yolks and a toasted English muffin on the side." If a customer changed his order, say from potato salad to coleslaw, the waitress would call, "hold that tater and make it slaw."

It was only after learning some of this diner lingo that Bloomie came to understand what she heard when she first entered the place. The waiter had called, "Check the ice," which was code for "look at the pretty girl who just came in." She was flattered by the compliment and enamored with the diner talk.

Back at her parents' eatery in Chelm's Pond, Bloomie tried to bring what she had learned into practice. The café was full one day when Rabbi Chayim Shmayim came in for lunch as he often did. Bloomie quickly found him a table and asked if he knew what he wanted. He briefly looked at the menu that Bloomie had written, in her best penmanship on the chalk board, and ordered the chicken soup. (Of course, with no *shokhet* in Chelm's Pond, and the cost of importing *kosher* meat so high, the chicken soup was fake. Bloomie's mother, Raizel, made it herself following her own special recipe. Even though it was all vegetarian she called it "chicken soup" anyway because, she said, "the recipe card was once in the same room as a chicken.") While Bloomie wrote down the order on her pad, she turned her head over her shoulder and called into the kitchen, "One chicken soup," and then went about her business, checking to see if the other customers needed anything.

From the other side of the café she noticed the rabbi waving her to come back. As she approached he said, "Bloomie, I've looked over the menu more carefully and changed my mind. I see that you have split pea soup today, and I'd like to have that instead." Eager to show off her new skills, Bloomie took out her order pad and pencil, found the rabbi's order slip, scratched out "chicken" and wrote "split pea." She turned to face the kitchen and called, "Hold that chicken and make it pea!"

The customers in the diner turned in shock to look at Bloomie and then, realizing what had happened, burst out laughing. Humiliated, Bloomie ran into the kitchen to hide. She knew the details of this incident would be repeated throughout the village. It was a long time before she regained enough self-confidence to use diner slang again. Nonetheless, she used every opportunity to visit other diners and restaurants and absorb the details of how they worked.

Geneva Bus Stop

During her rebellious teenage years, Bloomie took to making frequent trips to "see the world," though she never got more than several miles away. Despite her parents admonitions – and perhaps because of them – she secretly took up cigarette smoking. On one occasion, her parents thought to take advantage of her travelling spirit and sent her by bus to Flint, New York, where she was to visit the Empire State Potato Growers Association and obtain a special variety of potato that her parents could grow in Chelm's Pond and serve in their diner. The bus station nearest to Flint was in Geneva, on Route 20, seven miles away. Bloomie had to walk the rest of the way to Flint, but – ever prepared in her hiking shoes – she didn't mind.

After buying a sack of seed potatoes suitable for a short growing season and shallow, wet, nutrient-free soil, she walked back from Flint to the Geneva bus stop and joined the people gathered there, waiting for the bus. Impatient, Bloomie put down the sack of seed potatoes. With her left hand she took a cigarette from her shirt pocket and placed it between her lips. With her right hand she reached into another pocket, pulled out her prized Zippo lighter, and expertly spun the ridged wheel with her thumb. It didn't light. Annoyed, she removed the cigarette from her mouth, tossed it on the ground, took another from her shirt pocket, and dangled it from her lips. Angrily, she struck the lighter again, but it still didn't light. As the people at the bus stop looked on in amazement, she pulled the cigarette from her mouth, threw it on the ground in disgust, grasped another cigarette from her shirt pocket, and pressed it tightly between her lips. As she struck the lighter again, the young man standing next to her asked, "Excuse me miss, are you out of flint?"

Bloomie looked at him quizzically and replied, "No, I'm out of Chelm's Pond."

You wouldn't think a story like that would find it's way back to Chelm's Pond, but as it turned out, one of the people at the bus stop was a journalism student from nearby Hobart College who just happened to be Jewish. Her story was first published in the Hillel student newsletter and then reprinted in *The Jewish World*. The description she gave of Bloomie, "a lanky, athletic-looking, too-tall-for-her-age girl from Chelm's Pond, New York," was unmistakable. When copies made their way to Chelm's Pond, everyone laughed, asking Bloomie repeatedly if she was out of flint.

Wishing to avoid the embarrassment of any Chelmite in the future, the village council wisely passed a formal resolution: "If anyone in Chelm's Pond who smoked cigarettes travelled to purchase seed potatoes, they must never put down the bag of potatoes before lighting up."

The Rabbi's Hat

The Adirondacks are occasionally subjected to what meteorologists call microbursts – winds that touch only a very small area of land and last only a few seconds, but are so fierce that they can knock over trees. On an otherwise calm and pleasant day, Rabbi Chayim Shmayim was subjected to such a microburst. It blew the black felt hat right off his head. Eager to keep his head covered as required by Jewish law, he ran after it, but each time it came within reach, the microburst blew it away. Frustrated and out of breath, he began to despair. From inside Shlomo's and Raizel's diner, young Bloomie caught sight of his predicament. Seeing his frustration, she ran outside to join the chase. Just as the microburst was about to sweep the rabbi's hat far into the sky, she leapt up and caught it. She dusted it off on her apron, straightened out the brim, and graciously handed it to the rabbi. "Here you are," she said, "this is one black hat that did not fly away."

Rabbi Chayim Shmayim was so pleased and appreciative that he reached into his pocket, found two crumpled dollar bills, straightened them out, and gave them to Bloomie. Of course she refused, but he insisted. "I know you'll be going with your parents to visit relatives in Monticello," he said. "If you go to the racetrack, maybe you can make a bet and these two dollars will bring you luck."

Bloomie took the two dollars and – anticipating her success at the racetrack – promised, "I'll pay back your two dollars from my winnings."

Upon her return from Monticello, she went back to wait on tables at the diner. When Rabbi Chayim Shmayim came in for lunch he asked, "*Nu*, how did you make out at the racetrack?"

Bloomie looked happy and sad all at once. "I went to the racetrack," she replied, her voice faltering, "and looked carefully at the racing program. I noticed a horse in the first race by the name of Top Hat. The odds were 20 to 1, the longest shot in the field. But since you had given me the two dollars for saving your hat and the horse's name was Top Hat, I thought perhaps this was a divine message, so I bet on him. Almost immediately I felt I made a mistake, but there was nothing I could do about it. Then, an amazing thing happened. Top Hat, contrary to all expectations, came in First Place!"

"*Mazel tov!*" cried the rabbi, leaping from his seat in excitement. "You must have made a fortune!" Overhearing the excitement in the rabbi's normally staid voice, a few passersby eagerly popped into the diner to discover the news.

"Indeed I did, but there's more to tell," Bloomie continued. "I looked at the program for the next race, and saw a horse named Stetson. The odds were a long shot at 30 to 1. However, since you gave me the two dollars for saving your hat and Stetson is the name of a hat, I decided to bet all my winnings on that horse."

"*Nu?*" inquired the rabbi, anxiously. "What happened?"

"Stetson came in First Place."

"Oh Bloomie," exclaimed the rabbi. "That's wonderful!" And the Chelmites who had come in to hear the news were so impressed that they called out to others, "Come inside to hear about all the money that Bloomie won at the racetrack."

Bloomie continued, more nervous than before as the assembled listeners grew in number. "Race after race I followed the same pattern, betting all my winnings on the horse named after a hat. In the last race it seemed an even safer bet because the horse was the heavy favorite and his name was the French word for hat. So I put all my money on Chateau, but he stumbled and came in last and I lost everything."

Among the groans of the crowd that had gathered, someone called out, "Bloomie! 'Hat' in French is not chateau, it's chapeau!"

Bloomie hadn't realized her mistake and now she felt embarrassed and ashamed in front of the whole community. The Rabbi, who always tried to stick up for her, tried to protect her reputation by distracting the crowd's attention. He asked, "*Nu?* Which horse won?"

"Oh," she replied, "it was some long-shot Japanese horse named Yamika!"

The groans of the Chelmites could not have been louder, but not loud enough to drown out Bloomie's cries as she realized her own mistake. Rabbi Chayim Shmayim, imagining how devastated Bloomie must feel, held and hugged her as she sobbed. As everyone else left the diner, muttering about her foolishness, Rabbi Chayim Shmayim tried to comfort her.

"Don't feel bad, Bloomie. You know what we say, 'Some rely on chariots and some on horses ...'"[5]

---

[5] This is a reference to *Sefer Tehillim* (Book of Psalms) chapter 20, verse 7, which can be translated, "Some rely on chariots, and some on horses, but we remember the name of the Lord our God. The theme of relying on or trusting in God, rather than in man, can be found as well in Psalms 56, 62, and 146 (which is recited as part of the daily morning prayers) and in many other places in Jewish writings and elsewhere. All United States coins and currency bear its official motto, "In God We Trust."

The Way to Paradise

Bloomie's visits to various villages and natural areas led her to look unfavorably on her home town of Chelm's Pond, which seemed so ordinary and uninteresting by comparison. She surprised everyone with a poem she wrote in her senior year of high school.

Promise

A young man
bathed in soft sunlight
sits at a table in the park
absorbed in his studies

as silken seeds drift in the air
with the promises
of autumn afternoons

that winter days to come
will sparkle with fresh fallen snow
and winter nights glow warmly
in the company of those we love
that it can always be
just like this.

A bicycle leans on a tree
ready to take him
wherever he will go.

A tourist who was packing up after vacationing in Long Lake discovered that he didn't have enough room for his old motorcycle, so he had to sell it quickly. With $100 of her own money (nearly all of the waitressing pay and tips she saved over the years) and another $50 she borrowed from Rabbi Chayim Shmayim (which she promised to pay back) Bloomie bought it. The departing tourist said the motorcycle was reliable, but cautioned against going over 40 miles per hour. Bloomie named it *Merkabah*.

She had some difficulty passing the New York State motorcycle driver's license exam because she couldn't remember which was her "left" and which was "right." Then she met a woman with the same problem who said she had "dyslexia." She sometimes reversed the letters in words and confused right and left. Bloomie recognized that this must be the source of her problems learning both English and Hebrew – left-to-right, right-to-left, why can't they make up their minds! (As a student, when asked what miracle occurred when the ancient Israelites escaped from Egypt, she replied, "They learned Hebrew!") Bloomie was so pleased to find there were others that shared the same difficulties, she wanted them all to get together and support one another. She made a T-shirt that read, "Dyslectics Untie!" With new insight into her learning disability, she received special tutoring and was soon reading every book she could find.

When finally she passed the motorcycle exam, Bloomie's traveling increased, and while she made frequent trips to the local libraries, she discovered the villages and hamlets within a day's ride – places with cute names like Pudding Hollow, Pumpkin Hollow, Fairweather Corners, Podunk, and North Pole; Indian names like Oswegatchie, Ticonderoga, Wanakena, and Canajoharie; peculiar names like Ninety Six Corners, Coonrod, Hurlbutville, Cat Elbow Corners, and Spinnerville; and foreign names like Copenhagen, Antwerp, Norway, Peru, and Stone Arabia. However, she often got lost and had difficulty following maps. Her parents were so concerned that one day she wouldn't be able to find her way home, they bought her a refurbished GPS unit. Bloomie was so pleased that she immediately recorded the location coordinates for Chelm's Pond in the GPS as "Home," much to her parents relief. All she would have to do was touch "Home" on the GPS screen and follow the instructions.

After months of excursions, she became weary of the road and decided it was time to settle down. Much to her parents' disappointment, she had no desire to stay in Chelm's Pond. She wanted to make her home in the ideal place, a place that had everything. She consulted with Rabbi Chayim Shmayim, who – as much as he would miss her – encouraged her to follow her dreams and find her *Gan Eden*, her paradise. She liked that idea enormously.

She thanked the rabbi profusely, embarrassing him with a kiss on the cheek, and set off for the Tupper Lake library. There she sat down at one of the public computers, loaded the Internet browser, went to MapQuest, and searched for "Paradise." She was surprised to find that there were so many! However, she didn't think her little motorcycle would take her very far, so she chose the closest one, Paradise, New York. To her surprise, Paradise was only 10 or 15 miles south of Monticello, about 225 miles almost directly south of Chelm's Pond. Although she would rely on her GPS to get there, she printed out the directions as a backup.

It would be a five-hour trip along New York State Route 30 and local roads, since her little motorcycle could not handle the major highways. By the time she was ready for the big trip – checked *Merkabah's* brakes, battery, gasoline, oil, tires, and lights, sorted through her belongings to decide what few essentials to take and carefully packed them up in her saddlebags – it was already early evening. But rather than delay any further, she decided to leave Chelm's Pond even at that late hour. She would spend the night along the road and then conclude her trip in the morning. She said goodbye to her parents – who begged her one last time not to go – and to the rabbi – who now doubted the wisdom of the advice he had given her, as he contemplated a Chelm's Pond without Bloomie.

Bloomie rode her bike for a couple of hours until it started to get dark. With no money to spare, she passed the motel and diner and kept her eyes out for a convenient place where she could pull off on the side of the road and camp for the night. A wooded picnic area came into view off Route 30 just south of Amsterdam, about halfway to her destination. She pulled in, parked *Merkabah*, took out her sleeping bag, laid it on the ground, and ate the cheese sandwich and one of the wild dill pickles from the jar her mother had insisted she take for the trip. As she climbed into her sleeping bag she had a disturbing thought. *When I wake up in the morning, I'll be so eager to get to*

Paradise, I might take off in the wrong direction. Even though I have the GPS I might forget to turn it on and even though I have the printed directions I might forget to look at them. Wisely, she squirmed out of her sleeping bag and repositioned her motorcycle so that it faced towards Paradise. *Now all I'll have to do in the morning is jump on my bike and go.*

Tired from a long day, Bloomie fell right to sleep. Though a heavy sleeper, she was soon awakened by the roar of a half-dozen motorcycles, all pulling into the same picnic area. *A motorcycle gang,* she thought, *and me all alone in the night, far from the nearest house or business, and even further from my people.* She hoped they wouldn't notice her. But they did. Instinctively, she knew they were not members of *Hillel's Angels.*[6] She felt in her pocket for the copy her parents had given her of *The Traveler's Psalm.*[7]

"Now lookie here," called the leader, "we had ourselves a nice meal at that diner, and here we find ourselves a little dessert! Help yourselves, boys!" Poor Bloomie didn't know what they were talking about. All she saw as she looked up from her sleeping bag on the ground were the close-by headlights of several motorcycles, blinking out one by one as their riders turned off their engines. Since she had been the first one there, she felt they were infringing on her camping place, but then, thinking quickly – and given her good nature – she adopted the role of hostess whose duty it was to welcome her fellow travelers.

Bloomie quickly got out of her sleeping bag and stood up, much to the delight of the motorcyclists who now got a moon-lit view of her angelic beauty. As Bloomie surveyed their hungry looks, she remembered what the leader had said. "For a little dessert," she offered, "would you like one of my mother's delicious homemade wild dill pickles?" And with that, she opened

---

[6] An obvious play on *Hell's Angels,* this New Jersey motorcycle club takes its name from the renowned Jewish sage Hillel, who lived in the first century BCE. *Hillel's Angels* is a founding member of the Jewish Motorcycle Alliance.

[7] Psalm 121, sometimes referred to as *The Traveler's Psalm,* contains the verse, "The Lord shall guard your going out and your coming in, from this time forth and forever."

her jar of pickles and pushed one into each of their gaping mouths.

While the gang members crunched, chewed, and savored the best pickles they had ever tasted, Bloomie occupied their minds with confidently-delivered advice. "Now before you fellows settle in for the night, be sure to point your motorcycles in the direction you are traveling so when you wake up in the morning you won't head off the wrong way by mistake." Pointing to her motorcycle, she continued, "That's what I've done, see? Now I have a long day ahead, traveling to my new home in Paradise, so I'm going right back to sleep. Enjoy your pickles and have a peaceful night's rest." With that, she gracefully laid down in her sleeping bag, snuggled it close around her, and fell right back to sleep.

The gang had been too busy with their pickles to react, but now that they were finished, they felt cheated. They wanted more from this strange young woman than her pickles.

"Let's wake her up and have a party," said one of them.

Another, who was impressed by Bloomie's unassuming beauty and innocent self-confidence, said, "No, we should leave her alone."

A third, sensing the gang's restlessness, said, "I know, let's play a little trick on her."

"That sounds interesting," replied a fourth. "What did you have in mind?"

"Remember how she pointed her motorcycle in the direction she was travelling so in the morning she wouldn't take off going the wrong way? And then told us we should do the same? She must be some kind of a dimwit."

"Yeah, one who gives out pickles."

"Let's turn around her motorcycle so when she wakes up, she'll head off in the wrong direction!"

"That won't work, she has a GPS mounted on her handle bars. It will tell her she's headed the wrong way."

"Look here," said another, who was looking through her saddlebags. "She has directions from MapQuest."

And that's how they hatched the plan. Silently, they picked up her motorcycle and turned it around 180 degrees so it was pointing back to where she came from. They read the MapQuest directions and found out she came from Chelm's Pond and, as she had said, was heading to Paradise. They turned on her GPS and saw that "Home" was set to Chelm's Pond. They kept the location coordinates but changed the description from "Chelm's Pond" to "Paradise." Then they stoked up their campfire, laid

Bloomie's MapQuest directions on top, and watched as the paper curled into flames, flecks of its glowing-red remnants rising on the night air and disappearing into the stars above.

In the morning, they woke up early and greeted Bloomie with a hot cup of coffee. "We liked your pickles so much," the leader said, "we wanted to do something for you. You said you were heading to your new home in Paradise, so we changed the "Home" setting in your GPS so it will take you to Paradise instead of that other place you had in there."

Of course, Bloomie had mixed feelings about their taking such liberties with her personal property, especially since Chelm's Pond was not in the GPS database (how could it be, since it was merely a local place name, not a political subdivision or even a "point of interest" in a sightseeing guide, and was miles from the nearest road), and now the coordinates were lost to her and she might never find her way back. Nonetheless, she smiled pleasantly, still wary of these strangers. They watched eagerly as she packed up her sleeping bag and mounted her motorcycle. At the gang's insistence, she turned on her GPS and touched the "Home" button on the screen. They gave her big grins and waved wildly as she took off down the road in the direction her motorcycle was pointed.

Bloomie was justifiably relieved, but only partly so. She accelerated to the bike's top safe speed of 40 miles an hour, expecting at any second to see the motorcycle gang appear in her rearview mirror. Eager to put distance between herself and the gang, she continued to accelerate. At 50 miles an hour *Merkabah* began shake; at 60 miles an hour it began to wobble. She concentrated so hard on keeping *Merkabah* on the road that she didn't notice the similarity of the landscape as she traversed the same stretch of Route 30 that she had passed just the day before.

More than two anxious hours later, her GPS told her to slow down and turn off the main road. She was nearing Paradise. A mile or two more and the vague similarity of the passing landscape registered subconsciously in her mind. And when the GPS told her to leave the paved road and continue on a logging road and then a foot trail, the similarity could no longer hide itself. *Remarkable*, she thought. *So that's what Paradise is, a place where everything that's new seems like something you already know.*

When she came to a familiar looking cedar-shake cabin, she pulled over to the side. Her motorcycle screeched and sputtered to a stop, worn out and never able to start again. From the cabin emerged two old people who looked very similar to her mother and father. *But of course, they are 200 miles away back in Chelm's Pond,* she thought. The two people hurried over to see her, took her in their arms, and hugged and kissed her. *So this is what Paradise is like, where complete strangers welcome you warmly, without judging you, and are so glad to see you.*

She was very happy when the two old people offered her a job as a waitress at their diner, promising that one day, if she worked hard, she could become the manager and eventually the owner. Bloomie was very pleased and thought to herself, *Already I have been offered a job with clear opportunities for advancement. Now I can see why this place is called Paradise.*

It would be nice to end this story right here, showing how Bloomie saw something very familiar and yet appreciated it anew, and a nice, warm feeling of "there's no place like home." But that wouldn't tell the whole story. As the days went by, Bloomie continued to refer to the place as Paradise, to which the Chelmites responded, "You're *meshugeh*, this is no paradise." After several days of such confrontations, Bloomie became annoyed, and then angry, and then despairing. Paradise would be spoiled. Noticing her growing depression, her parents secretly talked to everyone in Chelm's Pond and asked them to accept – or at least ignore – Bloomie's geographical misperception.

Meanwhile, in an attempt to deal with her own distress, Bloomie confided in the local rabbi, who happened to have the same name and appearance as her good friend and supporter from Chelm's Pond. "This is Paradise," she insisted, "and all these people and places merely look like those I knew in Chelm's Pond. This is simply the nature of Paradise."

Rabbi Chayim Shmayim agreed. After all, if that was her idea of paradise, who was he to argue? Indeed he wondered, If I am Rabbi Chayim Shmayim in Paradise, then who is Rabbi Chayim Shmayim in Chelm's Pond? And if Rabbi Chayim

Shmayim of Chelm's Pond were to visit Bloomie in Paradise, how could the two rabbis tell themselves apart, how would they know which one should stay in Paradise and which one should return to Chelm's Pond? This caused Rabbi Chayim Shmayim, the oldest and wisest *khokhem* in all of Chelm's Pond, to turn his eyes to heaven for guidance – the habit that earned him his nickname, Shmayim – rising up on the toes of his right foot to get closer to heaven, reaching up and leaning so far to his right that he began to tip over, catching his balance just in time by crossing his left foot over his right, and in this fashion haphazardly hobbling across the valley and up and down the hills of Chelm's Pond in intense yearning for a solution.

After three days of searching, he fell asleep. He had a vivid dream, in which Rabbi Chayim Shmayim of Paradise was on a trip to Chelm's Pond. At the same time, Rabbi Chayim Shmayim of Chelm's Pond was traveling to Paradise. The two rabbis met in the middle and became confused. Which of them was which?

Since they couldn't remain forever at this halfway point in the middle of nowhere – well, strictly speaking they could remain there, but they both chose not to – they had to determine which one of them should go to which village. They stood back-to-back, closed their eyes, and turned around and around until they became dizzy. Then they opened their eyes and started walking, one heading to Chelm's Pond and the other to Paradise. That was the end of the dream. He was sure it was supposed to mean something.

The next day, he told his dream to Bloomie, though still unsure of what it meant. Bloomie's thoughtful gaze grew into her endearing smile as her eyes began to tear. "I don't know which Rabbi Chayim Shmayim you are," she said, "but I am glad you are here with me."

In the ensuing weeks, everyone accommodated the wishes of Bloomie's parents and made no fuss when Bloomie called the place Paradise, and Bloomie, in turn, offered no argument when someone referred to the place as Chelm's Pond. They were willing to accept each others foolishness, which might well be considered a step toward a genuine paradise.

Nonetheless, the Chelm's Pond Village Council had no desire for a repeat of this type of incident. After months of dialogue and thoughtful deliberation regarding several alternative proposals, they unanimously passed a resolution: "Effective today," they announced, "it is no longer permissible for anyone in Chelm's Pond to buy a motorcycle."

The Broiled Beet

Bloomie eventually reckoned with the fact that Chelm's Pond and Paradise were the same place, although she never figured out why. Nonetheless, and perhaps all the more, she worked hard in the diner and, as she grew older, her aspirations to become the manager and proprietor grew stronger. She felt the diner should have a clever and catchy name, like those of the more conventional eating establishments she had been impressed by in her visits to the neighboring villages. Names like the White Birch Café in Tupper Lake, or Marty's Chili Nights, the Mexican restaurant in Indian Lake, or Custard's Last Stand, the ice cream shop in Long Lake. And too, she wanted a name that was unmistakably and uniquely characteristic of Chelm's Pond.

Eat Here Now was descriptive, but too obvious (and worse, stimulated her parents to lecture her about someone named Ram Dass).[8] Her parents thought The Chelm's Pond Café had a nice ring to it, but Bloomie felt it was too ordinary. She liked Bloomie's, but her parents gave her a look that said, "What are we, chopped liver?" And Shlomo, Raizel, and Bloomie sounded like a law firm (although not a bad one at that).

Feeling frustrated, Bloomie looked for inspiration. She thought about the particular characteristics of Chelm's Pond. For one thing, everyone was highly learned and wise in even the most esoteric of Jewish law and custom. For another, they were too poor to hire a *shokhet* and couldn't afford to import kosher meat, so – with the exception of Raizel's homemade gefilte fish and Shlomo's Adirondack *Lox*® – the food in the diner was vegetarian. Being Jewish and vegetarian was not all that un-

---

[8] Ram Dass authored the 1971 book, *Be Here Now*, which influenced the hippie movement of the 1970s. He was born Jewish (his original name was Richard Alpert), but rejected Judaism. While his contributions to spirituality have been recognized, he has been criticized for his ignorance of Jewish intellectual and spiritual traditions.

common. In fact, Bloomie recalled, while the *Pesach seder* plate requires a roasted shank bone from a lamb or goat, it was a widely accepted practice for vegetarians to use a broiled beet.[9] Who in Chelm's Pond could afford to import a kosher shank bone? Everyone used a broiled beet. That was it. She named the café "The Broiled Beet." Moreover, rather than accept vegetarianism as the absence of meat, an unfortunate consequence of their isolated and impoverished condition, she would embrace it as an ethical, healthful, and environmentally conscious diet. The Broiled Beet would become a renowned gourmet vegetarian sanctuary in the midst of a backwoods culinary desert, boasting an inventive menu that combined traditional Eastern European Jewish tastes with the local food sources of the Adirondack Mountains. She would call it Adirondack-Ashkenazick fusion cuisine.

---

[9] This practice is based on a passage from the two-thousand-year-old *Babylonian Talmud, Tractate Pesachim*, 114b.

The Broiled Beet
Adirondack-Ashkenazick Fusion Cuisine
Meat-free, dairy-free, gluten-free, and taste-free specialties
The Finest Dining in Chelm's Pond

Kosher רשכ

Menu

Lumberjake Breakfast: A four-egg wild mushroom omelet* (cheddar or tofu "cheese" optional) complemented by a stack of *latkes* with applesauce, kasha pancakes with maple syrup, Shlomo's Adirondack Bagel & Lox® (cured brook trout on a pine-nut bagel; low-fat cream cheese, tomato, and onion optional), your own pot of our freshly ground, campfire-roasted, fair trade, high-mountain, shade-grown, burn-your-lip hot coffee, and a shot of Lake Placid Spirits *slivovitz*.

Chelm's Pond Fusion Sandwich: A sandwich of Raizel's homemade gefilte fish (fresh caught pike and chub from Chelm's Pond and Chub Pond) and creamy organic peanut butter (finely ground, gently roasted peanuts and sea salt) on your choice of rye (seeded, of course), whole wheat (stone ground), or our famous homemade gluten-free seven-grain bread (brown rice, sorghum, teff, millet, quinoa, amaranth, and corn).

Hillel Wrap: A layer of *kharoses* – Lake Champlain valley apples and Adirondack wild hickory nuts chopped and mixed with a sweet red wine from Lake George's Adirondack Winery – topped with a *shmir* of locally grown, freshly grated, sinus clearing khreyn (red or white) wrapped in a homemade organic gluten-free cornmeal tortilla.

Shlomo's "Why couldn't I have been Sephardic" Kitniyos Salad: A colorful and nutritious medley of *nahit* (aka *arbes*, chickpea, chana, garbanzo, or ceci beans), red lentils (aka orange lentils), and fresh corn served on a bed of organically grown, short-grained brown rice. Red pepper, cucumber, and beet greens round out this salad served with goldenrod-infused vinaigrette on the side.

The Broiled Beet
Adirondack-Ashkenazick Fusion Cuisine
Meat-free, dairy-free, gluten-free, and taste-free specialties
The Finest Dining in Chelm's Pond

Kosher רשכ

Menu

Raizel's Surf & Turf: Local high-in-omega-3 *shmaltz* brook trout & farm fresh, egg white* omelet with wild chives (in season), served with lightly wilted beet greens, a small boiled potato, and caraway seed sauerkraut on the side. Low-fat or non-dairy imitation sour cream optional.

Bloomie's Four Species Soup: Our seasonal fall special, just in time for Sukkos (but available year-round). *Barbúlyes*, *kroyt*, and *tzibele* simmered in a pumpkin soup base, topped with lightly roasted corn kernels and freshly ground black pepper. All from local sources.

Birthright Stew: A red lentil pottage that would make Jacob proud. A perfect complement to any meal or a meal by itself. Known to satisfy hunger. Caution: when ordering, avoid making life-altering choices. Cup or bowl.

Jack Benny Special: Half of a GAC (that's diner talk for a Grilled American Cheese sandwich, the "G" pronounced like a "J") on your choice of thinly sliced bread, only 39 cents. (If you don't understand why it's called a "Jack Benny" or why it's only 39 cents, ask someone who's older. A lot older.)

All meals served with a relish of *Raizel's Wild Dill Pickles*® and room temperature water (other temperatures available on request). Glass for your water: 25¢

* In gratitude for their service, our hens whose egg-laying capacities have run their course are accommodated for the remainder of their years at the *Chelm's Pond Home for Has-been Hens*.

Adirondack Mendel

You have become acquainted with the learned, honored, and beloved Rabbi Chayim Shmayim, the oldest and wisest *khokhem* in Chelm's Pond. You have gained some insight into the workings of the thorough, thoughtful, and decisive village council. Bloomie you have met, the loveliest, kindest, and sincerest *sheyne meydl* in all of Chelm's Pond. Even to her parents, Shlomo and Raizel, you have been introduced. *Shoyn genug?* It is time to present the central character of this story, although his reputation precedes him and he needs no introduction.

Astute readers will want to know how such a famous, capable, distinguished, and renowned adventurer, woodsman, mountain man, and Adirondack guide came to take up residence in such an isolated, irrelevant, insignificant, and inept community as Chelm's Pond. The answer is simple.

Deception

After Bloomie settled down in the Paradise known to others as Chelm's Pond, her parents expected that their daughter, the loveliest, kindest, and sincerest *sheyne meydl* in all of Chelm's Pond, would be the first to receive a marriage proposal. However, with each engagement of the other young women her age, their hopes dwindled. When she took over the management of the café and her ambitions became clear, they thought surely a promising young man would be enticed. But still, the marriage proposals went to others until no marriageable young men of Bloomie's age were left.

Sadly, Bloomie was not the only young woman in Chelm's Pond in this position. Her school-girl playmate and rival, Channie, was similarly unspoken for. Unbeknownst to the two young women, their parents conspired to pool their meager resources and place advertisements in the Jewish newspapers and on matchmaking websites.

"Two beautiful and wise young women seek two handsome and wise young men to build their lives together in beautiful and wise Chelm's Pond. Reply Box 613."

From the few inquiries they received, only two young men agreed to visit Chelm's Pond and introduce themselves to Bloomie and Channie. To avoid any bad feelings if one of the young men was to arrive by himself and choose one of the young women, thereby leaving the other to feel less worthy, the parents arranged to have the two men arrive on the same day, at the same time, on the same bus, so they could meet their future brides at the same time.

On the appointed day, the two young men, unbeknownst to each other, stepped off the bus at the hamlet of Blue Mountain Lake. One, a woodsman from up north, had a long, bushy beard and wore a long-sleeved white shirt, wide brimmed oilcloth hat, and ankle-high hiking boots. The other, a store clerk from Brooklyn, had a long, bushy beard and wore a long-sleeved white shirt, a wide-brimmed black felt hat, and well-polished dress shoes. Except for their hats and shoes, they could have been the same person!

When the woodsman got off the bus, he took a careful look around to get his bearings and immediately began his hike around Blue Mountain Lake, finding his way to Chelm's Pond with a trail map and the sun as his guide. When the store clerk from Brooklyn got off the bus, he took a careful look around, then got right back on the bus.

Meanwhile, in Chelm's Pond, the mothers of the two young women eagerly awaited the arrival of the potential *khossens*, the hoped-for grooms for their daughters. When only one man arrived, and they realized that the other would not be coming, they began to quarrel. "He's mine!" cried Raizel, Bloomie's mother.

"You're *meshugeh ahf toit*" yelled Channie's mother. "He's mine!"

"*Gey fayfn oyfn yahm*" screamed Raizel. "He's for Bloomie!"

On and on they argued until all of the Chelmites had gathered around, some taking sides, others offering unhelpful advice. Finally, someone sought out the rabbi and brought him to resolve the dispute.

The learned, honored, and beloved Rabbi Chayim Shmayim, the oldest and wisest *khokhem* in all of Chelm's Pond, soon arrived. Hearing the mothers shouting and cursing at each other, he immediately sought a solution to this heartbreaking conflict. He looked upwards for inspiration, extended his right arm as though to reach for an answer from heaven, and stretched out on his right foot to reach even higher. After a few moments in this inelegant position, he lost his balance, but caught himself by bringing his left foot around, crossing it over his right, and so he progressed in deep thought, unaware of his surroundings, searching for inspiration. Observing his efforts on their behalf, the mothers called a truce, confident that Rabbi Chayim Shmayim would soon arrive at a solution.

After three days, he fell asleep. In his sleep he dreamed that it was *Pesach* and he was leading the *seder*. He came to *yachatz*, lifted the embroidered napkin that held the three pieces of *matzah*, and removed the middle *matzah*. Suddenly he was awake. Immediately he sent for the mothers to meet him at the water pump in the center of the village. When he arrived the mothers were already there, along with nearly the entire village, electric with excited anticipation.

"I have the solution!" he announced as he made his way to the front of the crowd. The mothers quieted and turned to him expectantly, as did everyone in the assembled crowd. Rabbi Chayim Shmayim drew himself up to his full height. "We will cut the young man in half, and each of you will take home half of him."

Channie's mother was shocked. "Rabbi, that's ugly! You're more *meshugeh* than she is!"

But Bloomie's mother Raizel cried excitedly "Yes!" shaking her fist in affirmation. "Yes, cut him in half!"

Rabbi Chayim Shmayim, stretching out his arm and pointing his finger directly at Raizel exclaimed, "That is the true mother-in-law!"

And that's how the young woodsman came to Chelm's Pond and was designated for Bloomie.

The Fly Fishing Contest

Bloomie was *baroygis*. How dare her parents advertise for a groom without her permission, invite this man without her knowledge, and then fight over him – and win! She refused to talk to her parents, much less to this woodsman, this stranger, this *nishtgutnik*. She was angry at him for thinking he could just come into town and get her. She was angry at her parents for advertising and inviting in a strange man on her behalf. And, most difficult to admit, she was angry at herself for not having found a *boychik* on her own.

Upon learning of her feelings from Rabbi Chayim Shmayim, the woodsman appreciated Bloomie's plight and realized that it would be some time before she would have anything to do with him. He did get a good look at her, however, and if he knew any Yiddish he would have said she was a *sheyne meydl*. It would take some time before she would be able to put these circumstances behind her and get to know him. So he made inquiries, rented a room from Rabbi Chayim Shmayim, and planned to get to know the community.

Where should a newcomer go to mingle with the community? There were two obvious possibilities. He could go to the *shul* and attend the daily *minyan* or he could join the locals taking their meals at The Broiled Beet. He chose The Broiled Beet.

Bloomie avoided him, except to serve his meals. But, as the rare new person in town, everyone else wanted to know all about him. As a renowned adventurer, woodsman, mountain man, and Adirondack guide, he had plenty of adventures to share, and – unlike the *shul* – he easily attracted more than a *minyan*. In anticipation of hearing his after-dinner tales, Chelmites swarmed to The Broiled Beet like black flies to exposed flesh. Business boomed.

One day, after she had to rearrange the tables because everyone wanted to sit close by to hear his story, Bloomie heard someone ask, "Did you ever compete in one of those contests like they have at the Tupper Lake Woodsmen's Days?" Part of her wanted to listen to his story, but she was still angry. Everyone else sat expectantly, eyes and ears fixed on the woodsman, poised on their chairs. In spite of her feelings, Bloomie felt the need to understand this adventurer and listened intently, disguising her attention by cleaning tables.

"Oh yes, I used to enter contests all the time," he began, "but then I stopped. It wasn't fair, me winning all the time, so after I won the fly fishing contest, I gave them up so others could have a chance."

"The fly fishing contest," they all said. "Tell us about that one."

"There was a rich fellow from New York City who wanted to hire an Adirondack guide to take him fly fishing, and he wanted the very best fly fisherman there was, so he sponsored a contest. The winner would receive a cash prize and a lucrative yearlong contract to take him fly fishing. The rich man advertised and sent out mailings to all the Adirondack guides and even published a set of contest rules. When the guides read those rules, they realized this New York City man had a funny idea of what 'fly fishing' meant.

"On the appointed day all the Adirondack guides turned out to compete in the contest. The crowds of spectators were so great that the sheriff had to call in deputies from the five surrounding counties just to direct traffic, order three dozen Porta-Potties dropped in by helicopter so as to avoid a health and sanitation crisis, and establish an emergency hospital tent in the event that the severity of mosquito bites should make mass blood transfusions necessary.

"The first Adirondack guide came up to the platform." The young woodsman paused as he stood up tall and folded his arms over his chest. "His voice boomed over the excited throng. 'I am here to enter the fly fishing contest and my name is Mountain Manny.' The crowd went wild with clapping and cheering and whistling. Mountain Manny was well-known throughout the region and famous for his skills as an angler. He was big, too, over six feet tall and he weighed more than 200 pounds – before he ate breakfast. He took out his fly rod and laid it on the ground. He reached into his pocket and withdrew a matchbox. He opened the matchbox and revealed a stonefly.

Now, you know trout love those stoneflies. They make a pretty good meal for a fish, and they can be more than an inch long, maybe two. Mountain Manny released the stonefly into the still summer air and everyone lifted up their binoculars to follow it as it flew higher and higher. Mountain Manny picked up his fly rod and flicked it back and forth in careful, measured motions, let out nearly all of the line, and hooked that stonefly mid-air in a matter of just seconds. He reeled it in and proudly displayed it to the crowd, a smile from ear to ear and back around again.

"Well you never heard a crowd of people go so wild like they did that day. They wouldn't have believed it, except that they saw it through their own binoculars. Shaking their heads in disbelief, many of the other Adirondack guides just packed up and went home. Mountain Manny was getting ready to collect his prize and sign the fly fishing contract when another guide stepped up to the platform." At this, the young woodsman stood on top of his chair, causing all of the Chelmites to lean back in their chairs and crane their necks so they could see him. "He announced in a voice so loud it made the air shake, 'I am here to enter the fly fishing contest and my name is Giant Jim.' He stood there so tall he made Mountain Manny look like you were seeing him through the wrong end of your binoculars. That Giant Jim must have stood six foot ten inches tall and weighed 300 pounds. He really was a giant."

The Chelmites at The Broiled Beet pulled their chairs closer so they wouldn't miss a word, their eyes fixed on the young woodsman.

"He reached into his pocket, took out a matchbox, and released a mayfly. Now there isn't an insect the trout like more than a mayfly, even though they're only about a half-inch long. Everyone lifted their binoculars and followed that mayfly as it took off on a light summer breeze. Giant Jim took his time and looked through his fly fishing rods, carefully deciding which one to use, as the mayfly drifted further and further away. Finally, he selected a rod, picked it up, and gracefully flicked his wrist, letting out the line in long arcs – it was beautiful just to watch him, big as he was, gently working that rod and that big curving loop of line. Then, with a perfectly-timed flick of his wrist, the rod arced back, the line followed, and he hooked that mayfly. He reeled in the line and held that tiny hook between his fingers, showing off that tiny mayfly he had caught on the wing. The crowd erupted in applause accompanied by hootin' and hollerin' louder than a family of long-tailed cats in a room full of rockin' chairs.

"At this point the few remaining would-be competitors somberly packed up their fly fishing equipment and tried to look like they had never been there. The judge was about to award the prize to Giant Jim and have him sign the contract when I stepped up to the platform." Now the young woodsman stepped down from his chair and took his no-more-than-average-height stance in front of the crowd. "I said, in as big a voice as I could muster, 'I am here to enter the fly fishing contest and my name is Adirondack Mendel.'"

The Chelmites perched on the edges of their chairs, leaning forward so far that three of them fell over on their faces, but they were so entranced by the story that they didn't even feel embarrassed. Immediately they resumed their postures, listening keenly to every word.

"Mountain Manny and Giant Jim looked around trying to find me, seeing as I am much shorter than they and not so imposing a figure, until finally they looked down and saw me and – gracious gentlemen as they were – gave me some elbow room so I could enter the competition. I reached into my pocket, pulled out a matchbox, opened it slowly, and out flew a noseeum. Now, of course, you know that a noseeum is so-called because these blood-sucking, flying piranhas are so tiny you 'can't see them,' so everyone immediately raised their binoculars, turned the knobs to maximum magnification, and whipped their heads around to keep the little noseeum in view as it was buffeted around by the gusty summer wind. Meanwhile, I calmly picked up my fly fishing rod and in a few swift motions had the full length of line swooping back and forth from one end of the crowd to the other. Then, with one seamless movement of my arm and wrist, I was done, confident that I had displayed the greatest skill and won the contest. I reeled in my line, leaned my rod in the corner, and stood there proudly, my arms folded over my chest, ready to receive my prize and sign the contract.

"The crowd continued to watch the noseeum flit around in the wind and the judge seemed puzzled. He pointed to the wind and said to me, 'You made a great show of it, but the noseeum is still flying.'

"In reply, I declared, 'My dear judge, circumcision is not meant to kill.'

"And that's how I won the fly fishing contest."

The Chelmites, honored to be in the presence of this famous Adirondack guide, slapped him on the back, shook his hand, and wished him *mazel tov*. He acknowledged each of them by name and, to those he didn't know already, made a brief introduction. He was pleased to attract such a grateful crowd. But in the midst of all these admirers, Adirondack Mendel's eyes searched for the one person whose attention he most desired. Across the café he spied Bloomie as she cleaned a table, a charmed smile lingering on her face. But in the next moment, she caught him looking at her, and her expression turned to stone. *I'd better stick to my own business,* he thought, *and bide my time with Bloomie.*

Castle Rock

As a professional guide, it was essential for Adirondack Mendel to be intimately familiar with the particular wilderness areas for which he claimed expertise. He was not familiar with the area around Chelm's Pond so, if he was going to make his home here, he had to get busy. Every day after breakfast he would hike into the woods and head out in a different direction. He would explore the existing trails, climb to see the mountaintop views, locate the fishable waters, and be back at The Broiled Beet in time to share the tales of his adventures with the dinnertime crowd. Before long, he gained sufficient knowledge of the immediate area that he had to widen his exploration. At dinner one Sunday evening he announced that in the morning he would begin a longer trip so he could learn about the larger, surrounding area. He would not be back until Tuesday or perhaps Wednesday morning at the latest.

The Chelmites first refused to accept this news, then became angry. They tried to convince Adirondack Mendel that he had no need to make such a trip, and then – convinced of its inevitability, despaired. Finally, they resigned themselves to it. This was the first time Adirondack Mendel would be leaving Chelm's Pond since his arrival and they had grown accustomed to having his stories brighten their evenings. How could they return to hearing their own tired stories?

Nonetheless, the Chelmites gave him some parting gifts and wished him a successful journey and a safe return. Shlomo gave him an old aluminum pot and a serving spoon so if he came upon a *klezmer* troupe he would have something to bang and make music. Raizel gave him a Sherlock Holmes-type magnifying glass, big and round with a black handle to provide a firm grip, in case he had to read the potential side effects on a prescription label. Rabbi Chayim Shmayim gave him a large sheet of paper and a pencil so he would have something on which to write in case he had an inspirational thought. Everyone at The Broiled Beet that evening gave him a little something, except Bloomie, who purposely looked away, still angry. *Nisht geret iz oykh geret.* Her parents wanted to suggest that she give him something too, at least a word of encouragement, *halevai*, but feared if they did she would be even less likely to do so.

For the first leg of his trip, he climbed to the top of Castle Rock as he had once previously. He hiked up the relatively gentle north-facing slope and crossed the narrow summit to its southern edge. There he hoped to clear the trees that obstructed the view from the steep southern face, which he predicted would unveil a lovely panoramic view of Blue Mountain Lake. It would make a marvelous sight. Removing these treetops would be an arduous challenge for most people, but not for Adirondack Mendel.

From his backpack, he took his fifteen-inch, precision-honed, high-grade carbide-tipped, crosscut circular saw blade. Through the center hole of the blade he tied his 100-foot, abrasion-resistant, diamond-braided, dual-sheathed, lightweight, low-friction, moisture-shedding rope. He hurled the saw blade, like a frisbee, to the nearest tree. It felled the treetop in one high-torque spinning stroke. He pulled the saw back with the rope and repeated this procedure, taking careful aim at each tree. After the first ten or so, he started to get a little tired, and the bigger trees required two or three throws before he sawed them all the way through.

Now, excited as a toddler taking his first steps, he was going to try for the very first time, his new "yo-yo" method. He put a wooden dowel through the center hole of his circular saw so half of the dowel stuck out from each side. He wound the length of rope around one side of the dowel and a second rope of the same length around the other side. Holding the ends of the rope, one in each hand, he threw the saw out and watched as it spun, unfurling the winds of the ropes on the dowel and cutting down all the trees in its path, and when it reached the ends of the ropes, he yanked it back and it wound itself back on the ropes, ready to be yo-yoed out again. He liked this even better than the frisbee method. With his superb horizontal yo-yo skills, the saw blade never got stuck in any of the trees. If it had, he would have had to yank it out by the rope, or worse, climb the tree to free it. That would have made the job difficult.

After he had cleared about a hundred trees, just as he had anticipated, he could see Blue Mountain Lake with Osprey Island and Long Island and a dozen more islands and peninsulas, the mountains in the distance – Blue Ridge, Sugarloaf, and Round Top, and the blue sky with white clouds floating from horizon to horizon. A most magnificent view. (And if you don't believe me, go climb Castle Rock and see for yourself!) When he looked at his watch, though, he was disappointed to find that the job had taken him almost a full hour. He repacked his 100-foot, abrasion-resistant, diamond-braided, dual-sheathed, lightweight, low-friction, moisture-shedding rope and fifteen-inch, precision-honed, high-grade carbide-tipped, crosscut circular saw blade and turned to descend the mountain the way he'd come when he saw, charging toward him, a gigantic polar bear. He didn't have time to contemplate the impossibility of a polar bear in the Adirondacks, but had to decide what to do instantly. He could confront the polar bear and try to reason with it, or he could jump off the cliff he had just cleared. Wisely, he chose the 600-foot drop off the cliff down to the lake below.

As he made his vertical descent, he had an inspirational insight into the true meaning and ultimate purpose of life and withdrew from his pocket the sheet of paper that Rabbi Chayim Shmayim had given him. To keep the paper from blowing away, he had to hold it firmly with both hands, one on each edge and, so positioned, the paper produced sufficient aerodynamic lift that he glided down the mountain all the way from Castle Rock to the tip of Bluff Point, the peninsula that extended part way into Blue Mountain Lake, where he splashed to an abrupt and graceless landing at the water's edge. Now that he was on stable land, he reached into his pocket again and retrieved his pencil, but although he tried to remember, the excitement of the glide had disrupted his thinking and his inspirational insight vanished.

Not wanting to hike back up the mountain to recover the distance of his flight, and feeling a mite tired from his morning's work, he decided to make the rest of his way by water. He would paddle across Blue Mountain Lake, follow the other lakes and streams that connected it to Raquette Lake, and then flow down the Raquette River. All he needed was a paddle. And a canoe. Preferably a flat bottomed, lightweight model that he could float through the shallows and portage as necessary.

He rummaged through his backpack and found Shlomo's gift, the aluminum pot and spoon. Combing the shoreline, he quickly found a hand-sized rounded rock and another, larger rock half-buried in the ground. Using the half-buried rock as an anvil, he pounded the aluminum pot with the hand-rock, quickly shaping it into a one-man canoe. He had a preference for wood canoes, of course, but he didn't want to take the time to build one right now. A few strokes more and the spoon was transformed into a paddle. Checking the position of the sun in the sky, he was disappointed to see that it would soon be time for lunch. Eager to get on his way, he decided he would catch a fish for lunch as he paddled across the lake in his aluminum canoe.

Adirondack Mendel launched the canoe into the lake and sat cross-legged in the bottom. Paddling with his left hand, he used his right to pull Raizel's magnifying glass out of the storage pouch in his backpack. Peering into the water, he spotted a nice-sized lake trout and used the magnifying glass to focus the sunlight in the water just below the fish. Now you might think he would use that focused beam of sunlight to boil the water around that fish and cook it right there, but after using that technique several times, he had found it often overcooked the fish. Instead, he heated the water underneath the fish, producing a rapid upwelling that lifted the unwitting fish right out of the water. Adirondack Mendel merely reached out at the right moment and caught the fish in his right hand.

All the while paddling, his left arm had grown tired and it was time to switch hands. Simultaneously, he tossed the paddle with his left hand and the fish with his right from one side of the canoe to the other. As they crossed paths in the middle, the sharp edge of the twirling paddle cut two nice trout fillets. They landed in the bottom of the canoe where, with Adirondack Mendel's adept ministrations of the magnifying glass, they baked in the concentrated sunlight, augmented by a thin glaze of olive oil, a squeeze of fresh lemon, a minced clove of garlic, a few grinds of black pepper, and a garnish of finely chopped, fresh basil leaves. It was a delicious meal, undoubtedly the third best caught-cooked-and-consumed-in-a-canoe meal he'd ever had. Or maybe the fourth best.

Realizing now that his planned route and schedule were all *farblondzshet*, he decided to relax. What would he gain by getting all *farmisht*? He would get back when he got back; he might as well enjoy himself, however many days it took. Something interesting might turn up.

Aufruf the Dog

Leisurely, Adirondack Mendel paddled, poled, and portaged his way south and west to Raquette Lake, spending his nights under the stars. He continued north and east until he reached the Raquette River where he began to make his way downstream, a route that would eventually lead him back to Chelm's Pond. He did not expect to encounter any signs of civilization for miles, so he was surprised when he saw a cabin this far into the woods. Curious, he figured he would stop by the cabin to learn what he could, when he noticed a sign nailed to the front door, "Talking Dog for Sale." Puzzled, he knocked on the door and out came an old man. "The dog is tied up out back," he said. So Adirondack Mendel walked around the cabin to see a medium-sized dog, mostly black with some white markings, standing there, looking at him, smiling and wagging his tail.

"The sign says you can talk, but who would believe it even if it were true. So, can you?" he asked.

"I speak English fluently," the dog replied matter-of-factly, "and, although around these parts it doesn't pay, *a bissel* Yiddish."

Boggle-eyed, Adirondack Mendel stared down at the dog and staggered a few small steps backward. He had to lift up his jaw and catch his breath before he could say anything. "Astonishing! In all my travels and adventures never have I even heard of such a thing. How can it be?"

Taking this as the cue to tell his life story, the dog sat down, looked up at Adirondack Mendel, and began. "I discovered my linguistic gift while still a young pup. After reading the newspapers, I decided the best contribution I could make would be to help the government, so I emailed my application to the State Department, and in no time they interviewed me, gave me an IQ test, and put me on the payroll at the GS-5 salary level. They had me jetting from one country to the next, sitting inconspicuously in the same rooms with spies, agents, and world leaders who barely took note because no one imagined that a dog would be eavesdropping. I was assigned to work with General Colin Powell[10] when he was Secretary of State. That's when I picked up some Yiddish. He used to tell me, '*Gezunt dayn kepple*' – keep a healthy head. I realized that the time zone changes and jet lag were taking their toll on my 'healthy head' so I retired. I wish I could tell you about all of the medals I was awarded, but that would be a breach of national security. Now I'm spending my retirement years enjoying the natural beauty of the country."

Adirondack Mendel was excited. Without a moment's hesitation he walked back around to the door of the cabin and asked, "How much do you want for the dog?"

"Ten dollars."

"Ten dollars! Is that all? You're going to sell me that amazing dog who's risked his life serving our country so bravely for only ten dollars! Is there something wrong with him you're not telling me?"

"Yeah," the owner replied, "whatever he's been telling you – it isn't true. That dog is the most unreasonable, unmitigated, unconscionable, goldarndest liar."

That clinched it. Adirondack Mendel handed the man ten dollars and returned to the back of the cabin to fetch the dog.

As Adirondack Mendel untied the dog, he asked, "By the way, what's your name?"

"Aufruf," the dog barked.

Adirondack Mendel repeated, "What's your name?"

"Aufruf."

"Have you forgotten how to talk? Was it all my imagination? Tell me," he said again, patiently drawing out each word. "What – is – your – name?"

"I told you twice already. Aufruf. My name is Aufruf."

---

[10] Colin Powell is a retired U. S. Army four-star general who served the United States as National Security Advisor, Chairman of the Joint Chiefs of Staff, and Secretary of State. He credited his knowledge of "*a bissell*" Yiddish to his employment, while in high school, by Yiddish-speaking furniture store owner Lou Kirschner who told him, "*Gezunt dayn kepple*." ("Powell's Old Nabe Boss A Big Backer" by Michael Daly, *New York Daily News*, 8/2/2000. www.snopes.com/glurge/powell.asp)

"Oh, I thought you were just barking. What kind of name for a dog is that?"

"It's Yiddish. It means 'call up.' When Colin Powell wanted me, he used to yell '*aufruf*' and I would come. Before I understood any Yiddish I thought it was my name and it stuck." The dog smiled. "So, are you going to be my new owner?"

Adirondack Mendel got down on one knee and took Aufruf's head between his hands. "You are your own dog," he said. "We can be friends if you want and try to take care of each other. What do you say?"

"Do friends eat out of the same bowl?"

"For your sake, I hope not. I live with vegetarians."

"Vegetables. *Feh*. There was only one vegetable I ever liked."

"What was it?"

"Broiled beet."

"The Broiled Beet!" Adirondack Mendel suddenly stood upright. "We have to get going. I said I would be back by Tuesday or Wednesday morning at the latest and already it's Thursday." He ran back toward the river.

Aufruf kept pace easily, loping behind. "What's the big rush," he asked. "Got a hot date with the love of your life?"

"I don't know," Adirondack Mendel replied. "She won't even talk to me. But from what I can tell she is the loveliest, kindest, and sincerest beautiful young woman in all of Chelm's Pond."

"Chelm's Pond?" Aufruf's voice was incredulous. "Colin Powell used to tell me stories about the legendary fools of Chelm. When the angels were distributing souls they sprinkled the wise souls evenly all around the world, but the angel carrying the foolish souls made a blunder and dropped all of them in Chelm."

"It's the same people," said Adirondack Mendel. "They moved from Chelm in Poland when a real estate sharpie sold them a tract of land where, he promised, 'Every acre is two acres, you can till the soil with a teaspoon, and there are not only four seasons, there are five.'"

"*Oy vey. In drerd zeyer gelt.*"

Adirondack Mendel didn't have any idea what Aufruf was saying. "Maybe you could teach me some Yiddish."

They paddled, poled, and portaged down the Raquette River, up Pine Brook, and then bushwhacked their way south between Little Blue Mountain and Peaked Mountain. When they arrived in Chelm's Pond it was almost *Shabbos*. All the Chelmites were gathered at The Broiled Beet keeping a vigil for Adirondack Mendel, whose return was now more than two days overdue.

They were simultaneously relieved and angry when he arrived, but no one was more relieved and angry than Bloomie. "You inconsiderate lout," she cried out. "You *nishtgutnik!* You had the whole town worried, and all the while enjoying yourself without a care! You should have only one tooth in your head, and it should have a toothache, and you should have only stale *bagels* to eat." They were the first words she ever said to him. He was joyous. He looked at her with a smile and held out his arms to embrace her, but she folded her arms in front of her, turned her back to him, and stormed away. Adirondack Mendel started to go after her, but Aufruf stepped in his way and shook his head. No, this was not the time.

Adirondack Mendel Tells the Truth

Everyone left The Broiled Beet to go home for their *Shabbos* dinners. As Adirondack Mendel walked home with Rabbi Chayim Shmayim, the rabbi said, "You should come to shul tomorrow. I'll give you an *aliyah* so you can say the *Gomel* blessing, being thankful for your safe return."

"I can't," replied Adirondack Mendel.

"What, you don't know the blessing? I'll teach it to you."

"I still can't do it."

"What, you can't read Hebrew? Don't worry, I'll show you a transliteration."

"Sorry, Rabbi, I still can't do it."

"What is it then? Why can't you do it?"

Reluctantly, Adirondack Mendel replied, "I don't believe in God."

Rabbi Chayim Shmayim was not surprised. His conversations with Adirondack Mendel had prepared him for this admission, but this was the first time Adirondack Mendel had said anything so clearly to the point. "That may not be such an issue," the rabbi replied. "An old *midrash* says, 'If only they had forsaken me and kept My *Torah*.'[11] Studying the *Torah* and observing the commandments is more important than believing in God. Judaism is more concerned with behavior than belief."

Adirondack Mendel did not expect to hear such a thing, especially from a rabbi. Dumbstruck, he stared quizzically at Rabbi Chayim Shmayim, who continued. "We are *Ahm Yisrael*, the People Israel, the people who wrestle with God. Not every Jew believes in a personal God, a God who intervenes in the world. God can be an expression of our continuing appreciation of the wonder and mystery of all that was, is, and will be."

---

[11] *Pesikta de-Rav Kahane* 15:5; *Talmud Yerushalmi* (*Jerusalem Talmud*), Chaggigah, 1:7.

Adirondack Mendel recomposed himself and swallowed hard. "I still can't do it."

His impatience beginning to show, Rabbi Chayim Shmayim asked, "And why cannot you do it?"

There was a long pause, until Adirondack Mendel said, in a low, guilt-laden voice, "I'm not Jewish."

Rabbi Chayim Shmayim did not react immediately. In fact, he didn't say anything at all for the rest of their walk back to his cabin. He was trying to make sense of it all. He lit the *Shabbos* candles, recited *Kiddush*, said *Hamotzi*, and they started eating. Finally, he said, "So what are you doing in Chelm's Pond responding to an advertisement to be a groom for a Jewish bride?" Aufruf moved closer and perked up his ears. He wanted to hear this answer too.

"Well, I have never been part of a religion," Adirondack Mendel began, "although I certainly do marvel at the wonders of the world, the nature of the universe. And I have been curious about religion, and Judaism in particular, for as long as I can remember. I figured if I liked this young woman and she liked me, if necessary, I would convert."

"And do you know what we call a convert, a person who converts to Judaism?" asked Rabbi Chayim Shmayim, leaning toward Adirondack Mendel, his voice shrill. "Do you know, Mister Adirondack Mendel?"

"No," he replied, shrinking away.

"A Jew!" Rabbi Chayim Shmayim exclaimed, laughing and slapping Adirondack Mendel on the back.

"And what do you call a Jewish dog," asked Aufruf, presenting himself to the rabbi.

Apparently, this was the first time Rabbi Chayim Shmayim noticed the dog. "What's this? Did you bring this dog? Stop eating! We have to feed the dog first." At once, the rabbi got up from the table, removed a bowl from the cabinet, filled it with food, and placed it on the floor for the dog.

Much appreciative, Aufruf said, "*A groysn dank.*"

Without thinking, Rabbi Chayim Shmayim automatically replied, "You're welcome." Then it dawned on him. He had just said "you're welcome" to a dog. And then he came to the realization that the dog had said, "Thanks very much." In Yiddish no less! He turned toward the dog, his body rigid with trepidation and eyes wide with amazement. In a shaky voice, looking intently at Aufruf, he asked, "*Redstu Yiddish?* Do you speak Yiddish?"

"*A bissel.*"

Relieved that he hadn't been hallucinating, Rabbi Chayim Shmayim asked, "Where did this dog come from?" Before Adirondack Mendel could say a word, Aufruf gave him the *gantzeh megillah.* It was a long night.

The following morning, for the first time since arriving in Chelm's Pond, Adirondack Mendel accompanied Rabbi Chayim Shmayim to *Shabbos* services. He sat through the whole service, reading the English translations in the *Siddur.* Aufruf came too, posing as a service dog, and listened intently. Adirondack Mendel was surprised. He thought everyone in Chelm's Pond would be there, but there were not many more than a *minyan.* After services, Adirondack Mendel joined the Chelmites for *Kiddush* – a little wine, a little fish – it was very nice. All was forgiven and they wanted to hear about his recent adventures, but he was eager to pursue his own agenda. He politely helped himself to one last cookie and excused himself, hastening to The Broiled Beet where he hoped to find Bloomie in her apartment above the café.

Aufruf saw him leave the *shul* and followed after him. "What's your hurry? You couldn't throw me a *shtikl* pickled pickerel? What am I, chopped liver?"

"Sorry, Aufruf, I'm preoccupied."

"And what's preoccupying you is that young woman at The Broiled Beet, yes? I saw the way you looked at her last night. Let me tell you something, Mister Adirondack Mendel," he said, adopting Rabbi Chayim Shmayim's tone. "I saw the way she looked at you. I've had spy training and I know how to read people. Take my advice and let me do this."

"Let you do what?"

"Let me make the introduction. If there's anything a dog knows how to do, even ordinary, non-speaking dogs, it's how to introduce a man and a woman to each other. We've been doing it since Noah's dog."

"Okay. I haven't had any success so far, why not let you give it a try?"

They were almost to The Broiled Beet when Aufruf, pointing to a rustic log bench, said, "Wait here until I come back."

Aufruf continued down the short trail to The Broiled Beet, walked up the wood plank steps of the front porch, approached the door, and barked his name, "Aufruf."

In a few moments, Bloomie came down from her apartment above the restaurant, opened the door and came outside on the porch. Leaning down to pet his head, she greeted him. "You're a handsome looking dog, aren't you. What's your name, doggy?"

Wagging his tail wildly, Aufruf replied, "Aufruf."

"That's a lovely name for a dog. How appropriate. Who gave you that name?"

"Colin Powell."

"Hmmm. I don't know him. Is he your owner?"

"*Nisht ahin, nisht aher.* I am without an owner."

"You don't have an owner? But you have a collar!"

"Wait," said Aufruf. "Already I'm having some difficulty with this conversation."

"Oh? Why is that?"

"Look, I'm no young pup. I've been around, and I know too well how people react to me. Most people don't hear me talk because their brains are deaf to what their ears hear. A talking dog is simply an impossibility. When people do hear me, they are shocked. If they don't faint, they wonder if they have gone crazy. At the least, they are speechless. Even more rare is the person who overcomes the initial shock, only to be astounded that I can speak a word of Yiddish. But you! You're not surprised at all! And I am surprised that you're not surprised! How can you just talk with me like it was an ordinary thing?"

"Well, it is an ordinary thing for you, isn't it?" Bloomie replied. "And as for me, I talk to animals all the time."

"Yeah, but they don't talk back."

"Sometimes they do," Bloomie replied, and then added, slowly, for emphasis, "but you really have to listen."

Aufruf was taken aback. Here was a person who could teach him his own lesson. Perhaps he should be more open-minded to hear other animals. Maybe he wasn't the only one who could talk. On the other hand, his wiser self thought, if you really are so open-minded as to believe the unbelievable, why then, people might consider you a fool. Aufruf decided he really liked Bloomie. She was the loveliest, kindest, and sincerest *sheyne meydl* in all of Chelm's Pond, a *gutte neshomeh*. He thought for a moment longer and then asked, "Will you be my owner?"

Bloomie sat down on the porch steps so their heads were at the same level. She took Aufruf's head between her hands. "You are your own dog," she said. "We can be friends if you want and try to take care of each other. What do you say?"

Aufruf's jaw dropped, his eyes widened and teared up, he panted heavily, his heart pounded. Of course Bloomie noticed and asked, "What's the matter?"

With difficulty he responded, his voice raspy, "I have had many masters over the years and I have been trained and given orders by each, but what you just said I have heard only once before, and that from a young man only a few days ago."

"I would like to meet such a man," said Bloomie. "He sounds like the kind of person I could appreciate, and who could appreciate me. Do you know where he is?"

Aufruf hesitated for a moment, then regained his composure. "Yes I do," he said. And he walked down the porch steps from the front of The Broiled Beet and up the trail to the rustic bench where Adirondack Mendel waited.

In another village they might have said, "They were made for each other," or "The rest is history." But in Chelm's Pond they said, "It was *bashert*."

Economic Development

Adirondack Mendel continued his Judaic studies with Rabbi Chayim Shmayim all through the long winter months. That winter was very cold. Not so cold as in The Year of Two Winters, but cold nonetheless. How cold was it? It was so cold ...

> You could go ice fishing through the hole in a bagel.
>
> Even the *Shabbos* candles turned blue.
>
> Bloomie couldn't get into her apartment because her fingers stuck to the *mezuzah*.
>
> Rabbi Chayim Shmayim had an extra helping of *latkes* – just for the heartburn.
>
> Raizel, even while trying to raise funds for the *shul*, had her hands in her own pockets.
>
> To keep warm, everyone came to the *minyan*. (Now that's cold.)

After one of his overnight trips, Adirondack Mendel brought home a little gift, a novelty. He set it on the kitchen table in front of Rabbi Chayim Shmayim. It looked like a big snowball. "It was so cold last night," began Adirondack Mendel, "that my campfire froze. I wrapped it up in a snowball for you. Watch."

Rabbi Chayim Shmayim sat staring at the snow ball, his chin resting on his folded arms at the edge of the kitchen table. "*Nu*, what am I waiting for?"

"Wait, you'll see."

Gradually, the snowball melted, exposing a frozen fire. Suddenly, the flames licked into life. "You started a fire on my kitchen table!" Rabbi Chayim Shmayim shrieked as he quickly stood up and backed away.

"No I didn't," said Adirondack Mendel, smugly. "The fire thawed out and simply resumed burning. It's not good for anything but a little winter entertainment."

"*Ai-yi-yi*! Wait a minute, Mister Adirondack Mendel. There is more to this than you think. You could make a decent income selling these frozen fires to observant Jews. Instead of keeping a fire going all night long, which makes the house too warm during the summer, an observant Jew could simply defrost one of your frozen fires to warm some food. It would be *Shabbosdik* because you are not starting a fire, which is prohibited on *Shabbos*, you are merely resuming a fire that was previously created."

"Wow, a commercial use for frozen fires." Adirondack Mendel stroked his beard thoughtfully. "In the winter I could sell them as a back-up fire in case your regular fire should burn out, and in the summer I could sell them, like you said, as a way to have a fire on *Shabbos* without having to keep one burning the whole night and day. All I need are some good insulating containers to keep the fires frozen, and a good marketing campaign." And that's how Adirondack Mendel started in business, *farfroyren fayers far di frummies*.

But that wasn't his only new venture. Since he did not get much business as an Adirondack guide during the winter, Adirondack Mendel thought he would help out at The Broiled Beet. But business there slowed for the winter too, and another cook or waiter would be like putting ice on an icicle, so Bloomie asked him to fix some of the chairs and tables that were broken. They were fashioned in the Adirondack rustic style, chair and table legs constructed from tree trunks with the bark intact, and chair backs and support braces made from tree branches. Adirondack Mendel undertook to repair the chairs that were in need. He strengthened the back of a chair with branches shaped into a *Mogen David*. For another chair he made new arms in the shape of a *khes*. He replaced the broken legs of a table with new ones, each leg shaped like a *lulav*. Rustic/ Semitic Adirondack furniture was born.

Taking advantage of an old hop field – a left-over from when New York was a leading producer of hops – Adirondack Mendel started brewing beer. Even before his first batch was finished, he started to design a label for the bottle. He decided to name the beer in honor of Moses: Moishe Beer. His future father-in-law, Shlomo, had a better idea. "Name it after Moses' father-in-law," he said. The new label read, Yisro Ale.

Three days later the beer was ready to be bottled, and after two weeks more it was ready for tasting. Everyone in Chelm's Pond found the brew's hoppy taste to be exceptional. Already tasting the profit, Adirondack Mendel eagerly shipped a sample to the award-winning Adirondack Pub & Brewery in Lake George. He sent it with a letter imploring the brewmaster for his professional opinion. A week later the reply arrived: "Your horse has diabetes."

Conversion

Their budding relationship was coming into full blossom when Adirondack Mendel broke the truth to Bloomie that he wasn't Jewish. After a long pause, Bloomie opened her mouth to speak, then swallowed her words and pressed her lips together in grim consternation. In a panic and speaking as fast as he could, Adirondack Mendel explained to Bloomie his long-term interest in Judaism and his plan to convert. In fact, he was already studying with the rabbi, reading books, and learning about the holidays. He was working hard at learning to pronounce the "*khes*" in "Chayim." He had to admit that he was finding Hebrew to be extremely difficult. Aufruf, he was embarrassed to say, was learning it with ease.

While Bloomie could empathize with the problems of learning Hebrew, she was nonetheless troubled. "All my life, ever since I was a little girl, my parents told me, 'Bloomie, whatever you do when you grow up, do not marry a non-Jew.' Even though they didn't always observe *Shabbos*, even though they didn't go to *shul* on all of the holidays, even though they didn't keep everything in their kitchen kosher – on the rare occasions when they had the money to buy kosher meat they used the same dishes they used for dairy; when they bought a used pot they didn't always bother to *kasher* it. In spite of all that, they drilled it into me, 'Bloomie, whatever you do when you grow up, do not marry a non-Jew.' How can I face them now? What can I tell them?"

"Tell them I am going to convert before we get married."

When Bloomie told them, Shlomo and Raizel were forlorn. "*Oy vey is mir*, why did we bring that man into our world? It's our own fault."

Bloomie tried to comfort them. "Don't worry," she repeated. "I promise you, before we get married, Mendel's going to convert."

Adirondack Mendel was more than comfortable with Jewish ethics and practice – in fact he embraced them. At his prodding, Bloomie *kashered* everything in her apartment kitchen (most of her dishes, utensils, and appliances were hand-me-downs from her parents' not-completely-kosher kitchen) since that's where they would live after they got married. Of course, The Broiled Beet was strictly kosher in every respect, and although Bloomie didn't care much about the *kashrus* of her own private kitchen, she thought this was a harmless idea – only a pain in the *tukhus* – and saw no good reason not to comply with Mendel's wishes.

It was a tense two weeks after Bloomie broke the news about Adirondack Mendel's conversion that her parents invited both of them to dinner. This put Bloomie in an awkward position. "Sorry Mom and Dad," she said, "Mendel and I now keep strictly kosher, so we can't eat over at your cabin any more."

There was a long silence, and then Shlomo and Raizel, exasperated, yelled, "We told you not to marry a non-Jew!"

* * *

As Adirondack Mendel continued his preparations for his conversion, the other Chelmites helped by quizzing him on various topics, such as ... [12]

> Where in the *siddur* can you find the *Kiddush* for *Yom Kippur*?
> What is the appropriate *brakha* before eating a cheeseburger?
> On which days of *Purim* do we say *Hallel*?
> What *brakha* do you say after you light the *Shabbos* candles?
> How do you build a *sukkah* so the roof won't leak when it rains?
> Which prayer do you say to ask God to forgive you for being mean to a friend?
> On the Jewish calendar, does a new day begin at midnight or at sunrise?
> What is the kosher method for preparing a catfish?

---

[12] If you're not sure of the answers to these questions, see Adirondack Mendel's Study Guide.

How do you say "Hebrew" in *Ivris*?
What is the difference between *Shaleshudis* and *Seudah Shlishit*?
How do you make the *khes* sound so someone doesn't give you the Heimlich Maneuver and call the paramedics?
Which direction should you face when gossiping?

   His biggest difficulty was in learning how to read Hebrew – reading from right to left was awkward, recognizing the 27 Hebrew letters and twelve vowels was difficult, pronouncing the letter "*khes*" was challenging, and reading words was arduous and full of errors. To Adirondack Mendel's embarrassment, Aufruf made progress more quickly. Just by listening in on the lessons Aufruf learned the letters and vowels and became so proficient that soon Rabbi Chayim Shmayim was giving him his own lessons. As the winter months progressed, Aufruf mastered the *Birkhos Hashakhar*, the blessings that precede the *shakharis* service. One Sunday evening Aufruf made a proposal to Adirondack Mendel.

   "I have a way you can make some easy money," Aufruf began. "Tomorrow morning, let's go to the morning *minyan* early, and you take bets that I can lead the *Birkhos Hashakhar*. No one will believe that I can do it. You'll get great odds and make a lot of money." Adirondack Mendel had heard Aufruf studying with Rabbi Chayim Shmayim and knew he could recite the *Birkhos Hashakhar*, so he agreed.

   The following morning, as people put on their *tefillin*, Adirondack Mendel announced, "I'll bet anyone that my dog Aufruf can lead the *Birkhos Hashakhar*." They all thought Adirondack Mendel was a fool to make such a bet. Who had ever heard of a dog who could talk, much less say prayers in Hebrew. They were all willing to relieve Adirondack Mendel of a few dollars, and nearly everyone place a bet, a dollar here, five dollars there, five to one odds. When it was time, Aufruf advanced to the *amud* and stood on his hind legs. Adirondack Mendel was relishing his anticipated winnings, but Aufruf was absolutely silent. Adirondack Mendel prodded him, but nothing. After some embarrassing minutes, Herschel took over and, displacing Aufruf at the *amud*, began the *Birkhos Hashakhar*, his voice enriched by the knowledge that he had just won $25 from Adirondack Mendel.

After the service, Adirondack Mendel reluctantly paid off his bets while all the winners congratulated him on his foolish generosity. Afterwards, he took Aufruf aside. "What are you trying to do, drive me into poverty? You said you would lead the *Birkhos Hashakhar!* What are you doing to me?"

"Relax," said Aufruf, "just think what the odds will be on Thursday!"

* * *

Rabbi Chayim Shmayim asked Velvel and Malka, the two most knowledgeable and observant people in Chelm's Pond, to serve with him on the *Beis Din* to judge whether Adirondack Mendel should be permitted to convert to Judaism. They would ask him about his knowledge of Jewish laws and practice, his commitment to *mitzvahs*, his interests in learning more about Judaism, his expectations regarding his place in the Jewish community. Adirondack Mendel was confident of his responses in all these areas. The only question that concerned him was the one about God. He had long since told Rabbi Chayim Shmayim he was an atheist. On the appointed day, Adirondack Mendel sat in front of the *Beis Din.* He answered their questions with the confidence that comes from knowing the "right" answer and really believing it.

And then the inevitable question came.

"Do you believe in God?"

"No," Adirondack Mendel replied.

"*Nu*? What do you mean? Tell me more."

Adirondack Mendel felt defensive, but he didn't want to shy away from what he believed – and what he didn't believe. "I don't believe that there is a God who watches over us and listens to our prayers. I don't believe there is a God who intervenes in our lives or plays a part in world affairs, who favors one country or one people over another. I don't believe in using 'the will of God' as an explanation for things we don't understand – like why someone became ill, or why there was an earthquake, or how the world was created. I don't believe in a God who 'opens his hand and satisfies every living thing.'"[13]

A loud clump was heard as Velvel and Malka fell off their chairs. Shaking, they regained their seats. It was not only the content that shocked them. Never before had they heard Adirondack Mendel speak so seriously. Should they believe what he was saying? They bent their ears as Rabbi Chayim Shmayim, the oldest and wisest *khokhem* in Chelm's Pond, looked intently at Adirondack Mendel. "Let me ask you this. Do you believe that there is more to the world, to the universe, than we understand, and perhaps more than we will ever understand, but that it is somehow coherent and unified in how it works?"

"Yes, I believe that, and history shows that we continue to make more and more sense of the world – at least parts of it – and although we may never make sense of it all, it's only because we haven't figured it out, to the extent that we are capable."

"So you are an optimist! You believe that we will understand more about the nature of the world. And does that include the idea that we can make things better, more integrated, and bring about peace and good fortune for ourselves? What do you think of *tikkun olam*?"

"Yes," replied Adirondack Mendel, "I would call myself an optimist, but it's not a simple or self-confident kind of optimism. I believe that we have the potential to make things better not only for ourselves, but for all people and all living things, but sometimes we get it wrong and we make things worse. So we shouldn't be too confident in thinking that we know what will make the world a better place. We have to exercise doubt. When we hear an explanation, even if it seems to make a lot of sense, we have to keep our minds open to the possibility of another explanation. There is always another side to the story. 'Believe those who are seeking the truth. Doubt those who find

---

[13] Psalm 145:16. The psalm that contains this verse, *Ashrei*, is recited three times a day, in part because of this verse. Also, this line is part of *Birkas HaMazon*, Grace after Meals.

it.'[14] Nonetheless, it is our duty to work towards a better world, even though we might not see it done within our lifetimes."[15]

"And do you believe that Jews have a special obligation to do so, to be 'a light to the nations'?"[16]

"I do not think that Jews are necessarily more capable in making the world a better place – others may be just as capable or even more so – but as a people, as a community, we have taken on the mission to do so."

Malka and Velvel, listening intently to this conversation, were feeling more positive about Adirondack Mendel's conversion, but they saw that Rabbi Chayim Shmayim was not finished.

"I have one more question for you, Mister Adirondack Mendel." You could always tell, when the rabbi adopted that tone, that he expected to trump Adirondack Mendel's thinking. "When someone refers to God, when you read of God – obtaining justice for the oppressed, giving bread for the hungry, supporting the weak, the downtrodden, God who is gracious, kind, compassionate, merciful, faithful, loving, righteous – do you think God could serve for you as a metaphor for all of the connectedness and wonder and mystery of the universe and for all of the good intention and action to make the world a better place for all things?"

Adirondack Mendel leaned back in his chair pondering the question, while his left hand pulled at his beard. He sat forward and, looking first at Velvel, then at Malka, and finally at Rabbi Chayim Shmayim, replied, "Yes."

With the *bris* already completed (Adirondack Mendel was already circumcised but had a ritual circumcision for his conversion) the *Beis Din* observed his immersion in the *mikveh*, and his conversion was complete. Except for his name.

"It's not a requirement, but traditionally when a person converts they take a new name. So first, what is your real name?" asked Rabbi Chayim Shmayim.

---

[14] Andre Gide, French critic, essayist, and novelist (1869-1951), recipient of the 1947 Nobel Prize in Literature.
[15] *Pirke Avos* 2:21. Rabbi Tarfon said ... You are not required to finish the task, yet you are not free to withdraw from it.
[16] Isaiah, 49:6, 42:6.

"My real name?" he responded indignantly. "It's Mendel!"

"Mendel? I thought Mendel was just a name you used because you were responding to the advertisement for a groom to marry a Jewish girl."

"No, Mendel is my real name, the one my parents' gave me, that I've had all my life."

"But Mendel is a Jewish name. Didn't you know that?"

Adirondack Mendel was puzzled. "No, I had no idea."

"Why did your parents give you such a name?"

"I don't know. They never told me and I never asked."

"Well, Mister Adirondack Mendel, I think it's time you found out."

"But I haven't spoken to my parents in a long time."

"You mean you haven't even told them about your conversion? Your engagement? What kind of 'honor your father and mother' is that? *Nu?* Give them a call."

Adirondack Mendel had no reason to think his parents would object or be concerned. His parents did not practice any religion and he had never received any religious education. When, as a child, he had commented that he thought Judaism was interesting, all they said was, "That's nice."

So Adirondack Mendel hiked into Blue Mountain Lake to use a telephone. (Even if he had a cell phone it wouldn't be possible to get a signal in Chelm's Pond.) He called his parents and his mother answered.

"Mendez residence. Hello? Who's this?"

"This is your son, Mendel."

"Mendel! We haven't heard from you in so long. Let me get your father and put you on speaker phone."

"Mendel! This is your father. It's so good to hear from you. What inspired you to call?"

"I have a lot of news for you," Adirondack Mendel replied. "I've settled in Chelm's Pond, north of Blue Mountain Lake, I'm engaged to a young woman named Bloomie – the loveliest, kindest, and sincerest young woman in all of Chelm's Pond – and I've converted to Judaism."

There was a long silence. Adirondack Mendel started to get anxious. Then he had to hold the phone away from his ear as he heard both his mother and father shout in unison, "You can't convert to Judaism!"

"What do you mean, I can't convert to Judaism?"

"You can't convert to Judaism," they answered, their voices rising. "It's impossible! If your paternal grandfather, Mendel Mendez, after whom you are named, were to hear of this, he would turn over in his grave!"

Adirondack Mendel was shocked. He never expected this sort of reaction. "Why? Why are you saying I can't convert to Judaism?"

"Because you are already Jewish!" his mother replied. "We are descended from *marranos*, Jews who hid their religion and superficially converted to Christianity to avoid persecution. We have been hiding our Jewishness for 500 years!"

Adirondack Mendel had only one thing to say. "*Oy vey.*" It was the first time he said anything in Yiddish, and he didn't even notice.

After a moment's reflection, he became a little angry. "Why didn't you tell me?"

His father was the one who responded. "Look, Mendel, religions are full of *mishegoss*.[17] We didn't want to bring you up with pointless rituals, nonsensical rules, and irrational stories. It's like Karl Marx said, 'Religion is the opiate of the people.'"

"Well I don't agree," Adirondack Mendel replied. "That complaint is not properly about *religion*, it's about the unquestioning reliance on any particular version of reality or 'brand' of truth. It would be better to say, 'Systems of assumptions and knowledge unquestioningly believed to be true are the opiate of the people,' but for the sake of brevity, '*Answers* are the opiate of the people!' And Judaism is not about answers, it's about questions. It's not all *mishegoss*. It's three thousand years of history, ethics, laws, and customs, and stories that are even older than that. And yes, I will admit there is some *mishegoss*, maybe even a lot of *mishegoss*. But it's not someone else's *mishegoss*, it's your *mishegoss* – it's my *mishegoss*!"

Mendel's father was silent. He had no idea his son thought about such things or felt so strongly about them. And neither had Adirondack Mendel! Now all they had to do was make peace before the wedding.

---

[17] You might be wondering, why would Adirondack Mendel's father, a *Sephardic* Jew, express himself in *Yiddish* instead of *Ladino*, the language of the *Sephardic* Jews? And why would the *Sephardic* grandfather's name be Mendel, a *Yiddish* name? But that's another story.

Respect

Once they were officially engaged and had a date set for their wedding, Bloomie had a new worry. "Mendel," she confided, "I am worried that, even when we are married, we will not have any respect. Our fellow Chelmites will be polite to us, but inwardly and to each other they will think of us as fools."

"What are you talking about?" replied Adirondack Mendel. "Everyone here loves us."

"Yes, they think of us affectionately, but they don't think we are responsible, contributing members of the community. They think of me as a child who makes foolish mistakes. "

"But Bloomie," Adirondack Mendel implored, "all of your experiences have been valuable and you've learned from them. Good judgment comes from experience."

"And experience comes from bad judgment," Bloomie replied with an exasperated sigh. "What they remember is my bad judgment. And you know, Mendel, those stories you tell? I don't think everyone believes them."

Adirondack Mendel thought for a while and realized there was some truth to what Bloomie said. "So what do you think we should do? Should we move away?"

"I already tried that once, you know, and it didn't work. Now I have a different idea. You have to do something significant, something that will show that you can really make a difference, something that will earn everyone's respect."

"Why *me*?" replied Adirondack Mendel. "Why can't *you* do something like that?"

"Don't you understand?" Bloomie was nearly crying, her beautiful, imploring eyes filled with tears looking up at him. "When they see me they see the girl whose *khallah* is missing a braid, who could buy her *tefillin* at half price, who couldn't cut *gefilte* fish with a sharp knife. The fool who had a chicken pee in the diner, didn't know she was out of flint, lost all her winnings at the racetrack, thought she was in paradise. You are the one who has to make good for both of us, Mendel, for both of us – and for our children. We need the crown of a good name."[18]

For all her faults and shortcomings, Bloomie was the loveliest, kindest, and sincerest person Adirondack Mendel had every known, and he saw how this pained her. "I will do something," he promised, "but I don't know what."

"Neither do I." Bloomie sighed a great sigh – she was all *farklempt* – and sighed again, and then she brightened. "Let's ask Rabbi Chayim Shmayim."

Adirondack Mendel knew he could always find the rabbi at the morning *minyan*, and Rabbi Chayim Shmayim knew that when Adirondack Mendel came to the morning *minyan* it always meant that he had a question. It wasn't long after the last *amen* that Adirondack Mendel walked over to him. "Rabbi," he said, "Bloomie and I have a question for you. Can you join us for breakfast at The Broiled Beet?

"Your question must be serious indeed if it requires breakfast," smiled Rabbi Chayim Shmayim, but Adirondack Mendel did not smile back.

Bloomie brought over two breakfast specials – whole-kernel, organically-grown kasha cereal with maple syrup tapped from 200-year-old Adirondack sugar maples and a side of hard-boiled eggs from Bloomie's humanely-raised, cage-free, free-range, naturally-fed, retirement-guaranteed hens. Just as Bloomie sat down to join Adirondack Mendel and Rabbi Chayim Shmayim, she had to get up again to wait on some new customers, so Adirondack Mendel presented their problem to Rabbi

---

[18] "Rabbi Shimon said, there are three crowns: the crown of Torah, the crown of priesthood, and the crown of kingship. And the crown of a good name is superior to them all." ~ *Pirke Avos* 4:17.

Chayim Shmayim. He concluded, "So what would you suggest, Rabbi? What can I do that will gain the community's respect and relieve Bloomie's anxiety?"

The rabbi acknowledged the problem and dwelled on this question as he left The Broiled Beet. Once outdoors, he strained his uplifted eyes toward heaven as he rose up on his right foot, reaching ever higher. He teetered on tip-toe and lost his balance, preventing himself from falling down by stepping his left foot over his right to catch his shifting weight. Finally, after three days, he fell asleep, and in his sleep he had a dream. Suddenly he awoke and, delighted with his solution, rushed to The Broiled Beet to present it to Bloomie and Adirondack Mendel. "My children," he began, beaming with self-satisfaction, "here is what you should do." Rabbi Chayim Shmayim focused his eyes on Adirondack Mendel because, although the problem was felt most strongly by Bloomie, the solution centered on Adirondack Mendel. "At your *aufruf*, the Saturday before your wedding, in addition to being called to the Torah, you will be the *ba'al tefillah*. You will lead the congregation throughout the entire religious service."

While Bloomie looked tentatively pleased with this solution, Adirondack Mendel gulped as his face turned as white as a *Shabbos* tablecloth. "Rabbi," he finally choked out, "you're talking about a three-hour long service. And you know how much difficulty I have with Hebrew! I can hardly read a single prayer, let alone the whole service, and what good would it be, I don't even know what I'm saying. To me, they are just Hebrew sounds. There has to be another way."

"OK," said Rabbi Chayim Shmayim, "how about you lead only the *shakharis* service."

"But Rabbi," pleaded Bloomie, "no one comes to the *shakharis* service. You'll be glad if you get a minyan. Most people don't show up until *Aleinu*, and then only if there's a nice *Kiddush!*"

"You have a point," the rabbi conceded, as he felt the nearness of Bloomie's anxiety and hope. "Then lead only the *musaph* service!" He was pleased with his flexibility and insight in finding a workable solution. "You have a few months to prepare before your *aufruf*. You can announce in advance that the

Kiddush will be catered by The Broiled Beet and you'll be sure to have a good turnout. The whole community will be there."

"But Rabbi," interrupted Adirondack Mendel, still despairing of this mountain he would have to climb. "Even the *musaph* service is too much. It's too long. I couldn't do it."

After a few minutes of tense silence, Bloomie could no longer restrain herself. She began to sob, her brightest hopes fading to darkened shadows. Neither Adirondack Mendel or the rabbi could bear her anguish. "Rabbi," implored Adirondack Mendel, "please, please think of something different, something realistic, something I can manage."

For three days Rabbi Chayim Shmayim focused on nothing else, his face lifted closer to heaven than it had ever reached, his right leg extended from the very tips of his toes, valiantly stretching even higher, his heart longing for a solution. Hobbling diagonally across the valley and hills, everyone watched in wonder to see their learned, honored, and beloved Rabbi Chayim Shmayim, the oldest and wisest *khokhem* in Chelm's Pond, strive so earnestly to find a solution to even the most vexing problems. After three days, *oysgeshpilt*, he fell asleep and had the most vivid dream. The problem was solved.

He met Bloomie and Adirondack Mendel at The Broiled Beet for lunch. Bloomie brought him a *gefilte* sushi platter – slices of Raizel's homemade gefilte fish alternated with pickled carrot sticks surrounded by brown rice and rolled in a birch-bark wrapper with freshly ground, locally grown, eye-watering horseradish paste on the side. Eagerly, Bloomie and Adirondack Mendel sat down across from the rabbi to hear his solution. He was quite hungry and helped himself to a few pieces of the delicious sushi roll before speaking. He enjoyed their energetic expectation and relished it even more than the tasty *gefilte* sushi (which, in spite of its exotic origins, had a *Yiddishe tam*). His eyes were bright with anticipation as he pushed his plate to the side of the table. He took a sip of *esrog*ade, cleared his throat, and spoke.

"One prayer!" He paused for effect, aware of their misgivings, but feeling very satisfied with himself. "One prayer that will sum up in just one paragraph the entire *Shabbos* service!" He beamed. "The climax, the finale, the finest and most comprehensive prayer." He paused again. Of course, he knew what Bloomie and Adirondack Mendel wanted to know. They wanted to ask two questions at once: what was the prayer, and was he all *farblondzshet*. But they were too stunned to ask.

"I will help you learn it, Mister Adirondack Mendel," he continued with a look that clearly showed there was no opportunity for Adirondack Mendel to back out. "And you will learn not only the Hebrew, but you will learn the meaning. And as our sages have said, if you lead the prayer with *kavannah* and the congregation shares that meaning and intent with you, then perhaps, *im yirtzeh HaShem*, the prayer will have its intended effect."

"But I don't believe in prayer," Adirondack Mendel pleaded. "It's not meaningful to me."

Rabbi Chayim Shmayim reached for one of The Broiled Beet business cards at the end of the table. He took a pen from his pocket, turned the card blank side up, wrote something on it, and pushed it across the table.

Adirondack Mendel picked up the card and held it so Bloomie could see it too.

> The prayer
> changes
> the prayer.

"I don't get it," he said, looking at Rabbi Chayim Shmayim. "What does it mean?"

"Read it out loud," Rabbi Chayim Shmayim prompted.

"OK, but I'm not sure how to read it," Adirondack Mendel said. "I could read the first 'prayer' as referring to the written prayer that we read, and the second as the person who reads the prayer, the 'pray-er.' *The prayer changes the pray-er.* That would make sense if you think that a prayer has the potential to change the thinking or behavior of the person who says it."

"I thought it was the other way around," said Bloomie, moving closer to Adirondack Mendel so they could both stare at the little card more carefully. "I thought the first refers to the person – the 'pray-er' – and the second to the written 'prayer.' *The pray-er changes the prayer.* And that would be true because what the person brings to the prayer can change its meaning and intent."

"Come to think of it," Adirondack Mendel added, "you could read both as referring to the person. *The pray-er changes the pray-er.* One person who is saying prayers can affect another person who is saying prayers. Or, *The prayer changes the prayer*, as the meaning of one prayer can affect the meaning of another. So which is it?"

Rabbi Chayim Shmayim *kvelled* as he watched Bloomie and Adirondack Mendel, sitting so close together, studying the little card, tilting it toward one and then the other as one would turn a jewel to examine its facets. When they looked up at him inquisitively he said, "The answer to your question is – Yes! Keep an open mind. Now go learn the prayer."

Bloomie knew how difficult it would be. She took Adirondack Mendel's hands in her own and looked up at him pleadingly. "You can do it Mendel," she said, her voice breaking. "I know you can, and I'll do everything I can to help you." Now Adirondack Mendel was stuck. He could not see a way out. He was going to have to learn Hebrew, at least well enough to lead this one prayer, whatever it was.

"By the way," said Rabbi Chayim Shmayim, interrupting Adirondack Mendel's thoughts, "can you sing?"

* * *

The next day began the months-long marathon in which, in addition to all of the other preparations for the wedding, Adirondack Mendel, often with Bloomie at his side, spent every evening – except Friday – with Rabbi Chayim Shmayim, painstakingly learning the prayer, letter by letter, vowel by vowel, word by word, phrase by phrase, sentence by sentence, each with its meaning and intent.

To help his effort, Rabbi Chayim Shmayim gave Adirondack Mendel a copy of the prayer in Hebrew, another paper that gave a transliteration in English characters, and a third with an English translation. Bloomie took the three sheets of paper, cut them line by line, and pasted them together so Adirondack

Mendel could see each line in three forms, Hebrew, transliteration, and translation – all on one page. Studying this carefully, Adirondack Mendel did not learn just Hebrew sounds, he learned the Hebrew words and what each word meant. Bloomie suggested that on the day of the *aufruf*, they distribute copies to everyone in the congregation. "With this sheet of paper," she said, "any fool could follow the prayer."

"Yes," replied Rabbi Chayim Shmayim, "and anyone who is wise, even a wise fool, would not only follow the prayer, but really mean it. Your suggestion is excellent."

On the day of the *aufruf*, everyone in Chelm's Pond crowded into the little *shul*. Adirondack Mendel wore the *tallis* his father gave him, the same one worn by his ancestor when he left Spain hundreds of years ago and passed down generation to generation (although the *atara* had been replaced six times, the rectangular cloth, four, and the *tzitzis,* three). He was called up for an *aliyah* and recited the blessings before and after the *ba'al keri'ah* read the *Torah*. The whole congregation sang *Siman Tov u'Mazel Tov* and threw candy, and then the service continued as it did every Shabbos. Rabbi Chayim Shmayim led the *musaph* service, but towards the end of the repetition of the *Amidah*, something unusual happened. Rabbi Chayim Shmayim stepped away from the *amud*, and Adirondack Mendel took his place. You might think that no one would notice, and at first only a few did. But they immediately stopped their chatter and became silent, and the silence spread over the entire congregation. Bloomie walked down the aisle handing out copies of the prayer, which she had painstakingly rewritten by hand – in Hebrew, transliteration, and English – in beautiful calligraphy. In the silence, everyone waited, wondering what would happen next.

From the *bimah*, facing the *Aron Kodesh* – his back to the congregation – Adirondack Mendel sang slowly, drawing out each sound as Rabbi Chayim Shmayim had taught him.

Sim, sim, sim shalom.

In his mind, he summoned the celestial orchestra, and he could see the angels bringing their instruments, their tympanis and cymbals, and readying them, just as Rabbi Chayim Shmayim had seen in his dream.

Sim, sim, sim shalom.

He waited a moment longer for the angels of the chorus to arrive and arrange themselves in front of him, and then he sang out again, at a slightly faster tempo.

Sim, sim, sim shalom ba-olam, sim, sim, sim shalom ba-olam, tovah, uv'racha ...

And as he heard the celestial orchestra accompany him and the angelic chorus join him, he sang more brightly and eagerly and deliberately.

... kheyn, va-khesed, v'rakhamim – kheyn, va-khesed, v'rakhamim – aleinu v'al kol Yisrael a-mekha.

The whole congregation was taken by the unassuming forcefulness of his prayer, and they followed each word intently on the paper Bloomie had handed them, some seeing and really understanding their meaning for the first time.

Bar'kheinu Avinu kulanu k'ekhad, b'or pa-nekha.

As each phrase rang out, even the congregation could hear the celestial accompaniment, and each word a holy pronouncement.

Ki v'or pa-nekha na-sata lanu, Adonai Eloheinu, Toras khayim – Toras khayim – v'aha-vas khesed ...

And then, in voice that expressed gratitude and also confirmation.

... *utz'dakah, uv'racha, v'rachamim, v'chayim, v'shalom.* And again, even more emphatically. ... *utz'dakah uv'racha v'rakhamim v'khayim v'shalom.*

And in a powerful, climactic voice that was not rushed, a plea.

V'tov b'enekha l'varekh es am'kha Yisrael b'khol es, uv'khol sha-ah, bishlo-mekha.

He paused – composing himself and gathering together the energies of the angels above and the congregation below – and then concluded, first in a modest and plaintive tone.

Barukh Ata Adonai ...

Then shifted to a grand appeal, drawing out each word as the celestial tympanis, cymbals, and chorus joined in fullness.

... ha-m'varekh es amo Yisrael ...

And ended the prayer in a great symphonic appeal.

... ba-shalom.

Now I wish that you had been there so you could have judged for yourself because, you see, some people said that it was just another Adirondack Mendel tall tale, but others said that it really happened, that for the next ten minutes, over all the earth, there was peace.

* * *

From Chelm's Pond, centrally isolated in New York's Adirondack Mountains, just north of Blue Mountain Lake between Castle Rock and Little Blue Mountain ...

From Chelm's Pond, the steep valley where every acre is two acres, where you can till the soil with a teaspoon, and where there are not only four seasons, there are five ...

From Chelm's Pond ...

Zayt gezunt!

SIM SHALOM - שִׂים שָׁלוֹם

שִׂים	שָׁלוֹם	בָּעוֹלָם,	טוֹבָה	וּבְרָכָה
Sim	shalom	ba-olam,	tovah	uv'rakha
Grant	peace	to the world,	goodness	and blessing

חֵן	וָחֶסֶד	וְרַחֲמִים
kheyn	va-khesed	v'rakhamim
grace	and kindness	and compassion

עָלֵינוּ	וְעַל	כָּל	יִשְׂרָאֵל	עַמֶּךָ.
aleinu	V'al	kol	Yisrael	a-mekha.
upon us	and upon	all	Israel	Your people.

בָּרְכֵנוּ	אָבִינוּ	כֻּלָּנוּ	כְּאֶחָד	בְּאוֹר	פָּנֶיךָ,
Bar'kheinu	Avinu	kulanu	k'ekhad	b'or	Pa-nekha,
Bless us	Our Father	all of us	as one	with the light	of Your face,

כִּי	בְאוֹר	פָּנֶיךָ	נָתַתָּ	לָּנוּ,
ki	v'or	pa-nekha	na-sata	lanu,
for	by the light	of Your face	You gave	To us,

ה'	אֱלֹקֵינוּ,	תּוֹרַת	חַיִּים	וְאַהֲבַת	חֶסֶד,
Adonai	Eloheinu,	Toras	khayim	v'aha-vas	khesed,
Lord	our God,	the Torah	of life	and love	Of kindness,

וּצְדָקָה	וּבְרָכָה	וְרַחֲמִים	וְחַיִּים	וְשָׁלוֹם.
utz'dakah	uv'rakha	v'rakhamim	v'khayim	v'shalom.
and justice	and blessing	and compassion	and life	And peace.

וְטוֹב	בְּעֵינֶיךָ	לְבָרֵךְ	אֶת	עַמְּךָ	יִשְׂרָאֵל
V'tov	b'enekha	l'varekh	es	am'kha	Yisrael
May it be good	in your eyes	to bless	--	Your people	Israel

בְּכָל	עֵת	וּבְכָל	שָׁעָה	בִּשְׁלוֹמֶךָ.
B'khol	es	uv'khol	sha-ah	bishlo-mekha.
at every	season	and at every	hour	with Your peace.

בָּרוּךְ	אַתָּה	ה'
Barukh	ata	Adonai
Blessed	Are You	Lord

הַמְבָרֵךְ	אֶת	עַמּוֹ	יִשְׂרָאֵל	בַּשָּׁלוֹם.
ha-m'varekh	Es	amo	Yisrael	ba-shalom.
Who blesses	--	His people	Israel	with peace.

Note: Hebrew is written right to left. The transliteration and translation are presented word by word, so they too have to be read from right to left.

Glossary

Yiddish and Hebrew words and phrases used in the story are explained below. Most of the words are Yiddish. Hebrew words are indicated by (Hebrew) following the word. In addition, for Hebrew words, two transliterations are given in cases where there is a difference in pronunciation. The first is the *Ashkenazic* pronunciation, the second is the *Sephardic* pronunciation.

a bissel: A little bit.

a groysn dank: A big thank you.

Ahm Yisrael: The People of Israel. The underlying meaning of the word *Yisrael*, or Israel, is "wrestles with God." Jacob was given the name *Yisrael* after he wrestled with an angel of God (*Bereishis* (Genesis) 32:4–36:43).

ai-yi-yi: An exclamation of strong emotion.

Aleinu (Hebrew): A prayer that comes near the very end of the service.

aliyah (Hebrew): Literally, to go up or ascend. A person is called up to the Torah for an *aliyah* – to read the *Torah* or say the *brakhas* before and after the reading of the *Torah*. In a different context, it refers to the act of immigrating – going up – to the Land of Israel.

amen (Hebrew): Literally, so be it. An exclamation of agreement, said by listeners at the conclusion of a *brakha*.

Amidah (Hebrew): Literally, standing. The Standing Prayer. The central prayer of the Jewish religious service, the *Amidah* is recited in each of the three daily prayer services, and a fourth time during the *Shabbos musaph* service. It is also known as the *Sh'moneh Esreh* (eighteen) because in its original formulation it was composed of eighteen *brakhas*.

amud (Hebrew): The high table or lectern where the *ba'al tefillah* stands.

Aron Kodesh (Hebrew): Holy Ark. The special cabinet in a *shul* in which the *Torah* scrolls are stored. In most synagogues it is an integrated part of the eastern wall.

Ashkenazick: *Ashkenazic* refers to Jews from European lands. Their traditions differ somewhat from the *Sephardic* Jews from

Spain and North Africa. (Usually spelled with only a "c" at the end, I added the "k" only for symmetry with Adirondack.)
atara (Hebrew): Neckband of a *tallis*, usually ornamented.
aufruf: Literally, to call up. Customarily, an event that takes place on a *Shabbos* before a wedding when the groom is honored by being called up to read from the *Torah*. The event usually takes place in the *shul* of the groom's family (whereas the wedding usually takes place in the *shul* of the bride's family) thereby enabling the groom's community to share in the *simkhah* (joyous occasion).
ba'al keri'ah (Hebrew): Literally, master of reading. The person who reads from the *Torah*. Because the *Torah* scroll does not include the required vowels or musical notation, reading it indeed requires mastery.
ba'al tefillah (Hebrew): Literally, master of prayers. The person who leads the prayer service.
bagel: A bread in the shape of a ring (with a hole in the middle) about hand-sized. The dough is boiled before it is baked, which gives it a chewy texture and crisp crust. It probably originated in Poland and was popularized by Jewish immigrants to North America and elsewhere.
barbúlyes: Potatoes.
baroygis: Angry, furious, livid.
bashert: Destined to be.
Beis Din (Beit Din) (Hebrew): Literally, House of Judgment. A religious court of law.
Bereishis (Bereishit) (Hebrew): Literally, beginning. The title of the first book of the *Torah*, the *Five Books of Moses*. In English, the more widely used name for this book is *Genesis*, which is based on the Greek word that means origin.
bimah (Hebrew): A raised platform from which the *Torah* is read, located at either the center or the front of the *shul*.
Birkhos (Birkhot) Hashakhar (Hebrew): The series of blessings that marks the beginning of the communal morning prayers.
boychik: A boy or young man, usually meant in an endearing sense. (The "ch" is pronounced as in "chicken.")
brakha (Hebrew): Blessing. A prayer that expresses appreciation to God. There are specialized *brakhas* (*brakhot*) for particular things and occasions.

bris (brit) (Hebrew): Covenant. *Bris (brit)* commonly refers to the *bris milah (brit milah),* the covenant of circumcision, described in the *Torah (Bereishis* (Genesis) 17:9-14). It is performed on a Jewish male child when eight days old. A male who converts to Judaism must be circumcised. If he was already circumcised, the circumcision is ritually repeated by drawing a drop of blood.

Devarim (Hebrew): Literally, words. The title of the fifth book of the *Torah,* the *Five Books of Moses.* In English, the more widely used name for this book is *Deuteronomy,* which is based on the Greek word that means second law.

esrog, (etrog) esrogade (Hebrew): An *esrog* is a citron, a citrus fruit that looks much like a lemon, but larger. It is used ceremonially (along with the *lulav,* a palm branch matched with the branches of myrtle and willow) during the holiday of *Sukkos. Esrog*ade – made just like lemonade, but from citrons instead of lemons – is served, in season, at The Broiled Beet (and nowhere else).

farblondzshet: Fallen apart, disorganized, mixed up, confused, lost, bewildered, dysfunctional, impossible to put back in order.

farfroyren fayers far di frummies: Frozen fires for the very religiously observant. Available only from Chelm's Pond. Ruled to be *halakhically* acceptable by Rabbi Chayim Shmayim, a perfect gift for your *Shomer Shabbat* friends, only $13.18 each, $7.77 each for three or more (shipping and handling not included).Credit card payment accepted. Two day shipping available if ordered before 5:00 pm Wednesday.

fargesn: Forget.

farklempt: Heavy-hearted, oppressed-feeling, choked up with emotion.

farmisht: All shook up, befuddled, put off his game; dysfunctional, mixed up, confused.

fartumelt: Bewildered, dizzy, confused.

feh: An exclamation indicating distastefulness, disgust, disapproval.

Gan Eden (Hebrew): Garden of Eden.

gantzeh megillah: The whole, big, long (detailed, tedious, and boring) story. *Gantzeh* (Yiddish) means "whole." *Megillah*

(Hebrew) literally means "scroll" and commonly refers to the story that is written in the scroll or book.

gefilte: Deboned and ground or minced fish balls or patties having a uniform texture (that is easily cut with the blunt side of a fork). Typically made from a mixture of different fishes such as carp, mullet, pike, and whitefish.

gey fayfn oyfn yahm!: Literally, go whistle on the sea. Figuratively, get lost, leave me alone, don't bother me. (A cleaned-up version of the more typical *gey kakn oyfn yahm.*)

gezunt dayn kepple: Keep a healthy head.

Gomel (Hebrew): The *Gomel* blessing is recited in gratitude by a person who has returned safely from a dangerous or potentially dangerous activity or situation.

gutte neshomeh: Good soul. Gutte (Yiddish). Neshomeh (Hebrew).

halevai (Hebrew): If only.

Hallel (Hebrew): The series of Psalms (113–118) that are recited on holidays during the daily prayers.

Hamotzi (Hebrew): The blessing recited prior to eating bread, it is recited at the beginning of a meal and takes the place of reciting the particular blessing for each of the different types of food that make up the meal.

hock mir nisht kayn chaynik: Literally, "Don't chop me a tea kettle." Figuratively, "Don't beat around the bush," or "Don't chew my ear off."

im yirtzeh HaShem (Hebrew): If it is God's will, God willing. Literally, HaShem means "The Name," which refers to God's name without actually saying it.

in drerd zayer gelt!: Literally, "They put their money into the ground" (into hell). Figuratively, "They wasted their money."

Ivris (Ivrit) (Hebrew): The Hebrew word for Hebrew.

kasher רשכ (Hebrew): Literally, fit or proper. In conformance (or to bring into conformance) with Jewish dietary law (or in some cases, in conformance with other Jewish law). *Kashering* a kitchen goes well beyond a thorough cleaning of all food-related utensils and equipment and is subject to established regulations and standards. The anglicized form, *kosher,* might be used colloquially to indicate that something is proper or legitimate.

kashrus (kashrut) (Hebrew): The set of Jewish dietary laws. Also, how those laws apply to a particular type of food or situation.

kavannah (Hebrew): Concentration, intention, mindfulness.

khallah (Hebrew): A special bread, traditionally made with eggs beaten into the flour-dough mixture, made by rolling out the dough in three or more snake- or rope-shaped lengths that are then braided. It is typically baked for the Sabbath, other holidays, and special occasions. It commemorates the "showbread" displayed in ancient times in the Holy Temple as described in the *Torah* (*Vayikra* (Leviticus) 24:5-9). Often spelled *challah*.

khametz (Hebrew): During *Pesach*, Jews are not permitted to eat *khametz* – wheat, barley, spelt, oats, or rye – in any form other than *matzah*. Also, see *kitniyos*.

kharoses (kharoset) (Hebrew): A mixture of chopped apples, nuts, sweet wine, and other ingredients. It is one of the symbolic foods on the *Pesach seder* plate and is eaten as part of the *seder*.

khes (khet) (Hebrew): ח One of the letters of the Hebrew alphabet. The sound is produced by forcing air past the back of the tongue at the soft palate (without vibrating the vocal chords). It has the same sound as in the German *ach*. It appears in *Yiddish* and Hebrew in words such as *brakha, khallah, khokhem, and khossen*. To avoid confusion with the English "ch" sound, as in chair and child, the English transliteration of this sound is shown as *kh*. However, *ch* is used in some widely used English transliterations such as *Chayim* and *Pesach*. Phonetically, the sound of this letter is an uvular fricative. For more information, see *Adirondack Mendel's Study Guide*.

khokhem (Hebrew – *khakham*): Wise man. Surprising as it may seem, this term may be used sarcastically.

khossen (Hebrew: khatan): Groom.

khreyn: Horseradish.

Kiddush (Hebrew): Literally, sanctification. The prayer that is recited over a cup of wine to sanctify *Shabbos* and other holidays prior to the beginning of the meal at home or at *shul*. The

Kiddush that follows the Saturday morning prayer service is followed by the members of the congregation partaking of refreshments – ranging from wine and cake to a full meal – that is also commonly referred to as *Kiddush.*

kitniyos (kitniyot) (Hebrew): Literally, legumes. During *Pesach*, Jews are not permitted to eat *khametz* – wheat, barley, spelt, oats, or rye – in any form other than *matzah.* According to Ashkenazic tradition, this prohibition extends to *kitniyos*, which includes corn, rice, legumes, and *kasha* (buckwheat). For Ashkenazic Jews who are vegetarians, this prohibition leaves little vegetable protein in the diet. On the other hand, in Sephardic tradition, *kitniyos* are permitted.

klezmer: The traditional music of Ashkenazic Jewry, typically played at *simchas* (happy occasions) by traveling groups of musicians. From *klei zemer* (Hebrew), which means musical instruments.

kosher: Anglicized version of *kasher.*

kroyt: Cabbage.

kvell: To be full of pride and pleasure, to flow over with good feelings.

latkes: Fried potato pancakes.

lox: Salmon that has been cured in a brine of salt and other spices. Some varieties are smoked.

lulav (Hebrew): A palm branch matched with branches of myrtle and willow that is used ceremonially during the holiday of *Sukkos.*

marranos: In the 14th and 15th centuries, Spain became increasingly inhospitable to its substantial Jewish population. To escape hostility and oppression many Jews converted – voluntarily or under duress – to Catholicism; they were referred to derogatorily as *conversos* or *marranos.* Some converted only superficially and continued to practice Judaism in secret.

matzah (Hebrew): Unleavened bread, hard like a cracker. *Matzah* commemorates the speed with which the Israelites had to leave Egypt – they did not have time for the dough to rise to bake regular bread.

mazel tov (Hebrew): Literally, good luck. Figuratively, congratulations. An expression of pleasure at another's good fortune.

mensh: Good, decent person.

merkabah (Hebrew): Chariot.

meshugeh (Hebrew): Crazy, mixed up, confused.

meshugeh ahf toit: Literally, crazy unto death. Figuratively, really crazy, crazy as a loon.

mezuzah (Hebrew): A small scroll of parchment with prescribed verses from the Torah – *Devarim* (Deuteronomy) 6:4-9 and 11:13-21 – held in a case and attached to the doorpost of a building or room. The case is typically fashioned artistically from metal, wood, ceramic, or other materials.

midrash: An explanation of Biblical text, which may include narrative additions to fill in gaps in the Biblical story, that follows a traditional interpretive process.

mikveh (Hebrew): A ritual bath in which the body is fully immersed in water. A naturally occurring body of water can be used or – more typically – a bath house constructed specifically for this purpose.

minyan (Hebrew): The quorum of ten adults (traditionally males) required for the communal prayer service. The assembly of people who gather for the daily prayers is often referred to as the *minyan*. It is often difficult to get the required quorum, without which a few of the most sacred prayers cannot be recited.

mishegoss: Craziness, foolishness.

mitzvahs (mitzvot) (Hebrew): The commandments given in the Torah (all 613 of them, not just 10).

Mogen David (Hebrew): Shield of David, a six-pointed star shaped from two overlapping triangles.

musaph (Hebrew): The additional service on the Sabbath (and other holidays) after the reading of the *Torah*.

nisht ahin, nisht aher: Neither here nor there.

nisht geret iz oykh geret: Not speaking is also speaking.

nishtgutnik: No-good person, ne'er-do-well.

nu: "Well?" or "So?" A useful, flexible prompt for more information.

oy vey is mir: An exclamation indicating distress. Literally, "Pain is mine!" Figuratively, "Woe is me!"

oy vey: An exclamation indicating distress. Literally, "Oh pain!" Figuratively, "Oh my!" or "Oh no!"

oysgeshpilt: Exhausted, played out.

Pesach (Hebrew): Passover. The holiday that commemorates the escape of the Jewish people from slavery in Egypt.

Pirke Avos (Avot) (Hebrew): Literally, *Chapters of the Fathers.*" Translations typically bear titles such as *Sayings of the Fathers* or *Ethics of the Fathers*.

Purim (Hebrew): A Jewish holiday observed annually in the spring.

Redstu Yiddish?: Do you speak Yiddish?

Rosh Hashanah (Hebrew): The Jewish new year holiday. Literally, Head of the Year.

seder (Hebrew): Literally, order. The *Pesach seder* takes place in the home. It follows a prescribed order that includes the retelling of the story of *Pesach*, symbolic foods, and a full meal.

Sephardic (Hebrew): Jews from Spain, North Africa, and the Middle East.

Seudah Shlishit (Hebrew): The third meal, eaten on *Shabbos* afternoon. For more information see Adirondack Mendel's Study Guide.

Shabbos (Shabbat) (Hebrew): Sabbath, the seventh day of the week, the day of rest.

Shabbosdik: Appropriate for use on *Shabbos*.

shakharis (shakharit) (Hebrew): The daily morning prayer service.

Shaleshudis: The third meal, eaten on *Shabbos* afternoon. For more information see Adirondack Mendel's Study Guide.

shamayim (Hebrew): Heaven.

sheyne meydl: Beautiful girl.

shmaltz: Fat that is eaten, usually from animal fat.

Shmayim (as in Chayim Shmayim): Repeating a word with the first sound replaced by "shm" is a Yiddish device for making light of or diminishing an idea. Better known examples are "fancy shmancy" and "Joe Shmo."

shmir: Originally referred to cream cheese and now more broadly applied to various spreadable foods. For example, a *shmir* (of cream cheese or peanut butter) on a bagel.

shokhet (Hebrew): A person who is specially trained in the procedures required for the slaughter of animals according to *kashrus*, Jewish dietary law. The aim is to cause the animal as little pain as possible and to drain as much blood out of the animal as possible, since cruelty to animals and the consumption of blood are both prohibited.

shoyn genug: That's enough. Enough already. (Have you had enough already?)

shtikl: A small piece.

shul: Synagogue.

siddur (Hebrew): The Jewish prayer book, which contains the order of prayers for weekdays, *Shabbos*, and festivals.

Siman Tov U'Mazel Tov (Hebrew): Literally, "Good Signs and Good Luck." A joyous song that expresses good wishes.

slivovitz: A plum brandy that originated in Eastern Europe (and is still primarily distilled there). Popular among Jews from that region, especially during *Pesach*, because – unlike most spirits – it does not contain any *khametz*.

sukkah (Hebrew): A temporary one-room building that is erected for the holiday of *Sukkos*.

Sukkos (Sukkot) (Hebrew): An eight-day festival that celebrates the fall harvest. Also, see *sukkah, lulav, and esrog*.

takkeh: Really, truly.

tallis (tallit) (Hebrew): Prayer shawl. A rectangular cloth with *tzitzis* tied to each corner, worn while saying the morning prayers.

tam: Taste.

tefillin (Hebrew): Religious objects made of leather boxes that contain specific Biblical passages. There are two such boxes, one is worn on the arm, the other on the head, each held in place by leather straps. They are traditionally worn by adult males during the weekday morning prayer service. That Bloomie could buy them at half price implies that she wouldn't need one for her head. (*Nu?* Now do you get it?)

tikkun olam (Hebrew): Repairing the world. A requirement of Judaism that involves fulfilling commandments and performing acts of justice, compassion, and loving-kindness that contribute to making the world a better place.

Torah (Hebrew): Literally, teaching. *Torah* can refer to *The Five Books of Moses*, the handwritten parchment scroll from which *The Five Books of Moses* are traditionally read, or the whole of traditional authoritative Jewish teachings.

tukhus: Buttocks, bottom, rear end. From *tachas (tachat)* (Hebrew), which means under.

tzibele: Onion.

tzitzis (tzitit) (Hebrew): The fringes that are specially wound, knotted, and tied to each corner of the *tallis*. They remind Jews of their obligation to perform the 613 commandments. The numerical equivalent of the word *tzitzis* and the number of fringes, turns, and knots add up to 613.

yachatz (Hebrew): One of the prescribed steps in the *seder* in which the middle of three sheets of *matzah* is broken in half.

yamika, yamaka, yarmulke: A *yarmulke* (often pronounced *yamika* or *yamaka*) is the small round hat, referred to by some as a "skull cap," worn by Jewish males as a symbol respect for God. In Hebrew, *kippah*.

Yiddish, Yiddishe: Jewish. The *Yiddish* language (which is different from the Hebrew language) was spoken by Jews throughout Eastern Europe and was spread by those who emigrated. In addition to English names, Jewish children are typically given Hebrew or *Yiddish* names. In Chelm's Pond, people are called by their *Yiddish* names. *Yiddishe* is the adjective form of *Yiddish*.

Yom Kippur (Hebrew): The Day of Atonement. The holiest day of the year that culminates the Ten Days of Penitence or Days of Awe that begin with *Rosh Hashanah*. *Yom Kippur* is a fast day during which no food or drink is consumed.

Yisrael: See Ahm Yisrael.

zay gezunt: Literally, be healthy, be well. Figuratively, goodbye. *Zayt gezunt* is the plural form.

zekher tzadik livrakha: may the memory of the righteous be a blessing.

Adirondack Mendel's Study Guide

Editorial note: It took some time for Adirondack Mendel to find answers to the "helpful" questions that appear in the *Conversion* chapter. As a service to students of Judaism everywhere, he compiled these answers. With his permission I am reporting them here. He insisted I add the following disclaimer:

If you already know the answers, these questions are funny. (OK, mildly amusing.) But if you don't know the answers, as I didn't, you don't get the humor and you go searching for answers. And it's an odd day when the questions are funny, but the answers are serious – and sometimes complicated. Anyway, here are some answers, at least partial answers. Like most Jewish questions, there are multiple answers and follow-up questions. If you want to know more, you'll have to look them up for yourself.

Where in the siddur can you find the Kiddush for Yom Kippur?

You will find the *Kiddush* for *Shabbos* and all the other holidays, but you won't find the *Kiddush* for *Yom Kippur* in the *siddur* – or anywhere else. *Yom Kippur* is a fast day, so unlike other holidays, there is no *Kiddush*.

What is the appropriate *brakha* before eating a cheeseburger?

There is a specific *brakha* to be said before eating any food, even a snack. The *brakha* you would say before eating cheese is the same as the one you would say before eating a burger. But you would never say a *brakha* before eating a cheeseburger, because you would not eat a cheeseburger! The laws of *kashrus* prohibit eating milk and meat together. (Of course, if you ordered a burger at the Broiled Beet, it would be a veggie burger, so having cheese on it would be OK.)

On which days of *Purim* do we say *Hallel*?

First, the holiday of *Purim* is only one day long. (In rare cases of an ancient walled city it might be celebrated for two days, and when the second day falls on *Shabbos*, for three.) Second, although *Hallel* is said on *Pesach, Shavuos, Sukkos,*

Shemini Atzeres, Simkhas Torah, Chanukah, and *Rosh Khodesh* (the start of every new month), it is not said on *Purim.*

What *brakha* do you say before you light the *Shabbos* candles?

You say ... *lehadlik ner shel Shabbos* – to kindle the light of *Shabbos*. Now, the tricky part. The rule for every *brakha* is that you say it and then immediately perform the act. However, for Ashkenazim, saying this *brakha* signals the beginning of *Shabbos*, and on *Shabbos* you are not permitted to light a fire. So, if you recited the *brakha* and then lit the candles, you would be violating Jewish law. Instead, the practice among Ashkenazim (and some Sephardim) is to light the candles – but not look at them, put the match aside, cover your eyes, say the *brakha,* and then uncover your eyes and discover that the candles are already lit! So for Shabbos candles, you say the *brakha* <u>after</u> you light them.

How do you build a *sukkah* so the roof won't leak when it rains?

The roof of a sukkah must be made of vegetation – for example, tree branches, palm leaves, bamboo sticks – and must be constructed so the roof material is open enough that by day you have more shade than sunlight, and by night you can see the stars. If it rains, you get wet.

Which prayer do you say to ask God to forgive you for being mean to a friend?

You can ask God to forgive you for a wrong you committed against God, but if you want forgiveness from a friend, you have to ask your friend.

On the Jewish calendar, does a new day begin at midnight or at sunrise?

The new day starts at sundown. The Jewish calendar follows the moon. The new moon marks the beginning of a new month. Every two or three years there is an additional month so that the lunar calendar remains roughly in sync with seasonal changes and the solar year.

What is the kosher method for preparing a catfish?

For a fish to be kosher, it must have both fins and scales. The catfish does not have scales, so it's not kosher, no matter how it might be prepared.

How do you say "Hebrew" in *Ivris*?

This is a little bit like asking, "What was the color of George Washington's white horse?" The Hebrew word for Hebrew is *Ivris*.

How do you make the *khes* sound so someone doesn't give you the Heimlich Maneuver and call the paramedics?

"To pronounce the guttural *kh* (technically known as the 'uvular fricative') pretend you are trying to expel a fishbone that is stuck in the roof of your mouth."[19] Lest someone think you are really choking, you can produce this sound by forcing air past the back of your tongue at the very back of the roof of your mouth (the soft palate), without vibrating your vocal chords. Try this procedure until you get the hang of it.

1. Sit in a chair and relax.
2. Close your mouth and swallow.
3. At the end of the swallow, make note of the position of the back of your tongue against the back of the roof of your mouth.
4. Keep your tongue in that position and open your lips.
5. Exhale somewhat forcefully.
6. As you practice, you can produce the sound by exhaling less forcefully.
7. Add a vowel sound after the *kh* and you have it made.

What is the difference between *Shaleshudis* and *Seudah Shlishit*?

When I heard one person say *Shaleshudis* and another say *Seudah Shlishit*, I had no clue they were saying the same thing. Both refer to the third meal, eaten on *Shabbos* afternoon. There are regional variations in the pronunciation of Hebrew and Yiddish, just as there are in English (for example, a Boston versus a New York accent, or American versus British or Aus-

---

[19] Leo Rosten. *The Joys of Yinglish.* McGraw Hill, 1989, p. 2.

tralian). The most notable difference in Hebrew pronunciation is between the Ashkenazic (European) and Sephardic (Spanish, Portuguese, and Northern African) regions, and the most notable difference in pronunciation is of the letter ת (*tav*), which can also appear with a *dagesh* (dot) תּ. Ashkenazim pronounce תּ (*tav* with a *dagesh*) as the letter "t" and ת (*tav* without a *dagesh*) as the letter "s." Sephardim pronounce both forms as the letter "t," with the ת (*tav* without a *dagesh*) having a softer sound. For this reason, two forms of transliteration are given for the Hebrew words in the Glossary.

Beyond that, this particular example demonstrates other regional differences. *Shaleshudis* condenses two words into one, reverses their order (adjective-noun, as in Yiddish, rather than noun-adjective, as in Hebrew) and is pronounced with the accent on the first syllable of each word, as in Yiddish, rather than on the last, as in Hebrew.

Which direction should you face when gossiping?

When Jewish people pray they face the direction of *Yerushalayim* (Jerusalem). When Jewish people gossip, they violate Jewish law.

About the Author and Illustrator

Sandor (Sandy) Schuman

My father was a storyteller. It was his everyday way of communicating ideas and values. I followed his example, incorporating storytelling in my work as an educator and organizational consultant, but I didn't realize it until several years ago. After leading a three-day training program, I read the attendees' evaluation forms. In response to the question, "What did you like best about the program?" several people responded, "Sandy's stories." I didn't understand what they were talking about until my co-trainer pointed out several stories I'd told. Since then I've told stories more intentionally and in public performances where I tell personal adventures, historical sagas, tall tales, and Jewish stories. I am pleased to share my stories with you. Find out more at www.exedes.com/stories

Kevin Kuhne

Kevin Kuhne received a BS in Art Education from SUNY New Paltz in 1977. He left full time teaching in 1984 to pursue a career as a chef, but has never stopped painting and drawing, and continues part-time to teach adult education as an art teacher and as a tutor for Literacy Volunteers of America. He and his wife raised two wonderful boys who were supplied with constant storytelling through an immense collection of children's and adult literature. Every holiday, birthday, minor event, or free evening was an excuse for creating illustrations for each other, a tradition that continues to this day by long distance mail.

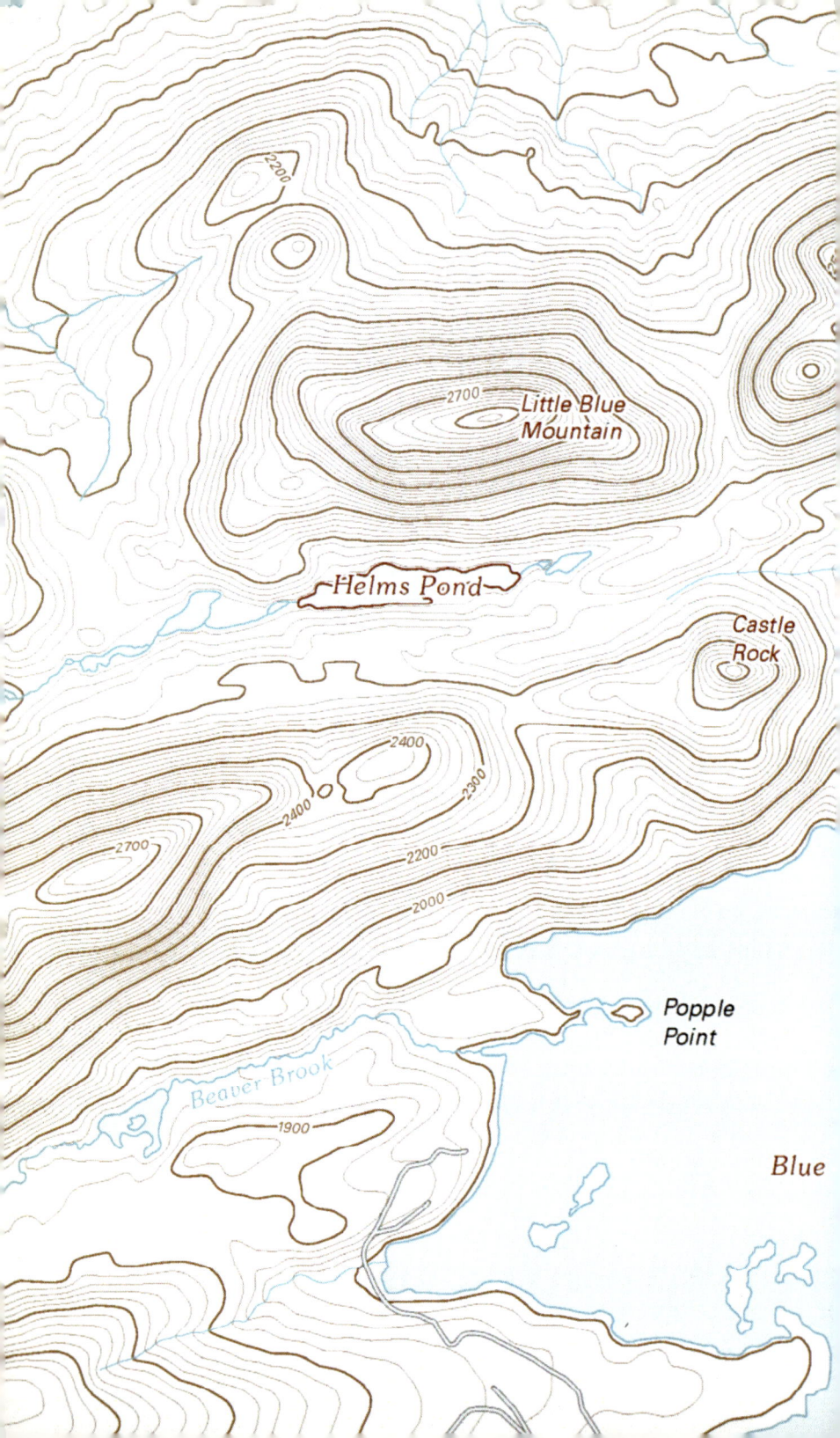